Für Dieter

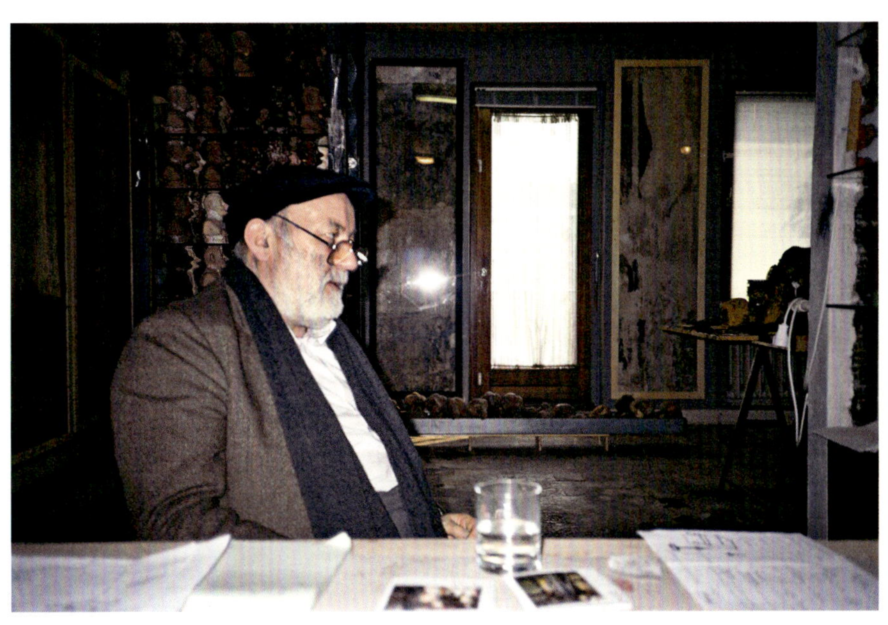

Dieter Roth vor *Selbstturm* im ‹Schimmelmuseum›,
Hamburg, 13. November 1994.
    Dieter Roth in front of *Self Tower* at the Schimmelmuseum (Mould Museum),
    Hamburg, 13 November 1994.

Dieter Roth

Die Zeit vergeht, das Leben scheints ebenso

Time passes, so does life, it seems

Fotos und Dokumente
zusammengestellt und herausgegeben
von Beat Keusch und Erika Streit

Photographs and documents
compiled and edited
by Beat Keusch and Erika Streit

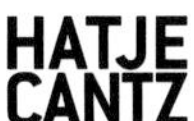

8 Vorwort
9 Foreword

12 Im ‹Schimmelmuseum›
At the Schimmelmuseum

68 Im ‹Roth-Raum›
In the Roth Room

78 Auf Island
In Iceland

100 ‹Chez Donati›
Chez Donati

Unter den Fotografien in diesem Buch von Beat Keusch und
Erika Streit sind noch nicht veröffentlichte Dokumente aus
dem ‹Schimmelmuseum› in Hamburg und dem ‹Roth-Raum›
in Basel – beides Langzeitprojekte meines Vaters, an denen
ich über fünfzehn Jahre hinweg gearbeitet habe. Sie zeigen
den lebendig-prozessualen Aspekt dieser Skulpturen.

Als Beat und Erika zu ihrem ersten Islandbesuch
kamen, den Dieter mit so viel Freude vorbereitet hatte, war
gerade Winter und überall Schneegestöber … Verloren im
weissen Nichts reisten wir glücklich durch eine Landschaft,
die wir nicht sehen konnten. Dieters Plan für diese Reise
und die Fotos dazu werden in diesem Buch ebenfalls gezeigt.

Im letzten Teil des Bandes ist die Ausstellung zu
sehen, die ich zusammen mit Beat als Hommage an meinen
Vater nicht in einem Museum, sondern im ‹richtigen Leben›, im Restaurant ‹Chez Donati› in Basel, eingerichtet hatte.

Beat und Erika standen meinem Vater sehr nahe.
Sie waren etwa zwanzig Jahre lang befreundet. Wann immer
er in Basel war, haben sie sich getroffen. Es gab viele Gemein-
samkeiten zwischen ihnen. Diese Freundschaft besteht
mit mir weiter.

Seyðisfjörður, Island, September 2020

Björn Roth

The photographs in this book edited by Beat Keusch and
Erika Streit include hitherto never published documents from
the Schimmelmuseum in Hamburg and the Roth Room in
Basel—two of my father's long-term projects that I worked on
for over fifteen years. They reveal the living-emergent
aspect of these sculptures.

When Beat and Erika visited Iceland for the first time
—a visit Dieter had been preparing for with much joy—
it was deep winter and there was driving snow everywhere…
Lost in the great white nothingness, we happily travelled
through a landscape we couldn't see. The book also contains
the itinerary and photos of this trip.

The last part of the volume features the exhibition
that Beat and I organized as a homage to my father, notably
not in a museum but in a real-life setting, namely in the
restaurant Chez Donati in Basel.

Beat and Erika were close to my father. They were
friends for roughly twenty years. They met up whenever my
father travelled to Basel. They had so much in common.
This friendship lives on in me.

Seyðisfjörður, Iceland, September 2020

Björn Roth

Wer ihn zudem als Mensch gekannt hat, weiss, wie Kunst und
Leben in ihm ein Einziges waren, dass er ein Poet in allem war,
auch in den Bereichen seines Tuns, die vom Kunstpublikum
unbeobachtet blieben.

Who also knew him as a person was aware that, for him,
life and art were one, that he was a poet in everything he did,
including the things that went unnoticed by the art public.

Jan Voss

Am 23. April und 13. November 1994 lud uns Dieter Roth
nach Hamburg ein ins ‹Schimmelmuseum› und in das benach-
barte ‹Dieter Roth Museum›. In Zusammenarbeit mit
seinem Sohn Björn und weiteren Isländern hatte Dieter Roth
eine zweigeschossige ehemalige Remise in eine begehbare,
sich ständig verändernde Skulptur, das ‹Schimmelmuseum›
verwandelt. Im Aussenbereich wuchsen Pflanzen und
entstanden *(Abfall-)Objekte,* im Innern sah und roch man
Arbeiten aus Schokolade, Zucker und Gewürzen. Die Pflanzen
im Aussenbereich gehörten ebenfalls zur Installation, wie
die Polaroidporträts von Besuchenden und deren Aufzeich-
nungen in den Gästebüchern. Die bei unseren Besuchen
entstandenen Fotos haben Dieter Roth sehr gefallen, weil sie
das Kunstwerk ohne Inszenierung zeigen, so wie man
es bis 2004 erleben konnte.

On 23 April and 13 November 1994, Dieter Roth invited us
to Hamburg to the Schimmelmuseum and the neighbouring
Dieter Roth Museum. Together with his son Björn and
friends from Iceland, Dieter Roth had turned a former, two-
storey coach house into a walk-in, constantly changing
sculpture, the Schimmelmuseum. The outdoor area was a
space with growing plants and emerging *(Waste) Objects,*
inside there were works made of chocolate, sugar, and spices
which you could not only see but also smell. The plants in
the outdoor area as well as the polaroid portraits of visitors
and their entries in the guestbooks were also part of the
installation. Dieter Roth loved the photographs we had taken
on our visits because they showed the authentic installation without additional frills, just as visitors could experience
it until 2004.

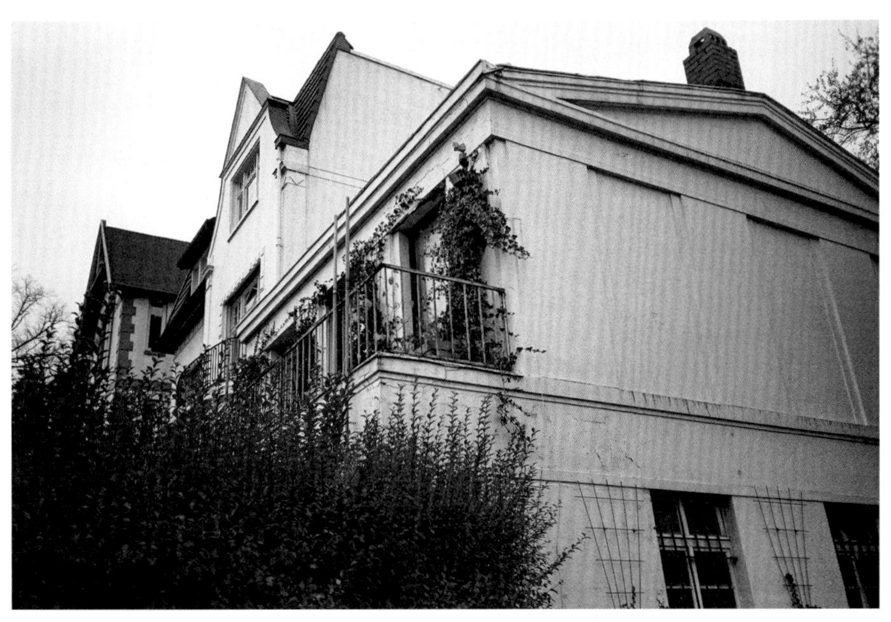

Das ‹Schimmelmuseum› an der Alsterchaussee 40 in Hamburg bestand von 1992 bis 2004.
The Schimmelmuseum at Alsterchaussee 40 in Hamburg existed from 1992 to 2004.

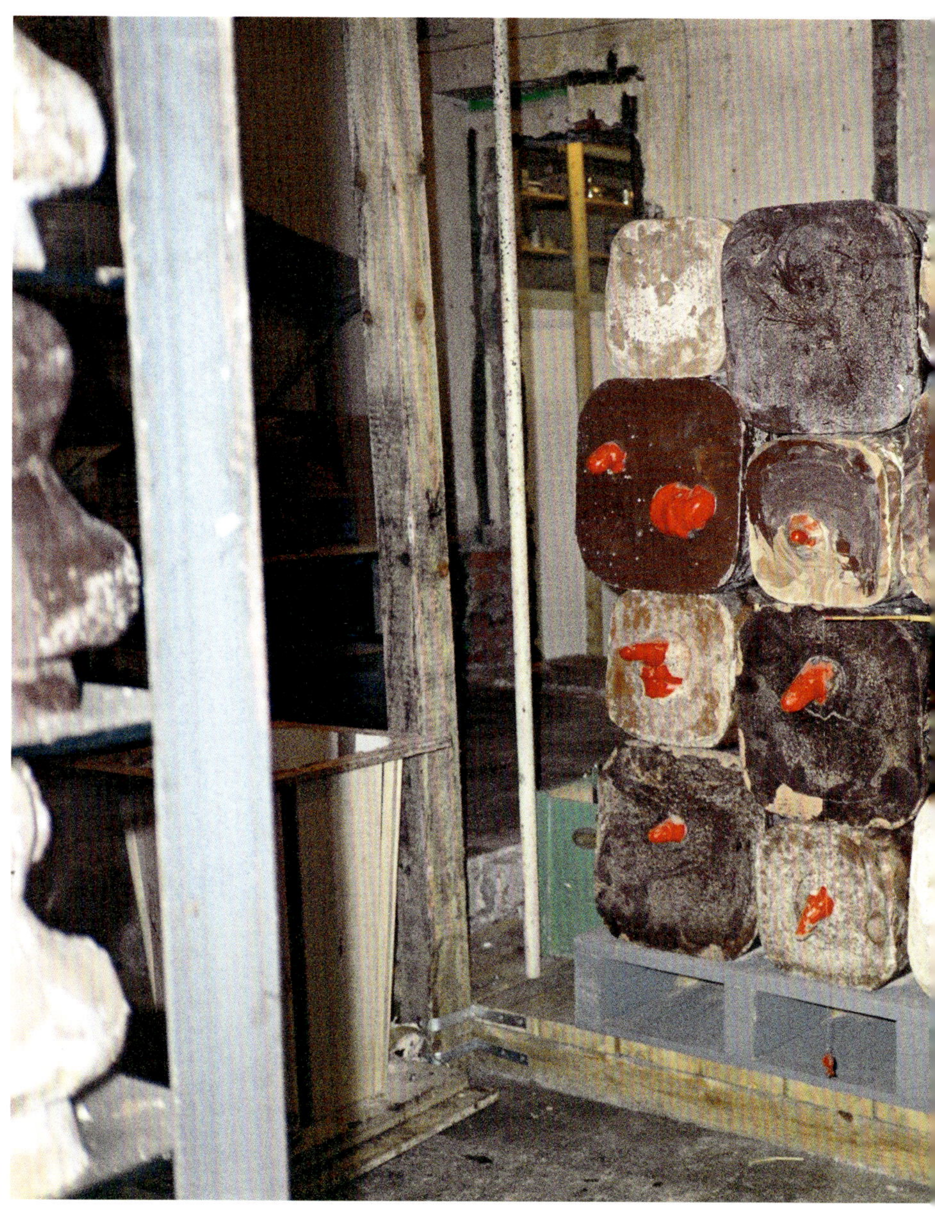

Coquillen-Zwerge, Kunststoffgartenzwerge in Schokolade eingegossen.
   Coquille Gnomes, plastic gnomes cast in chocolate.

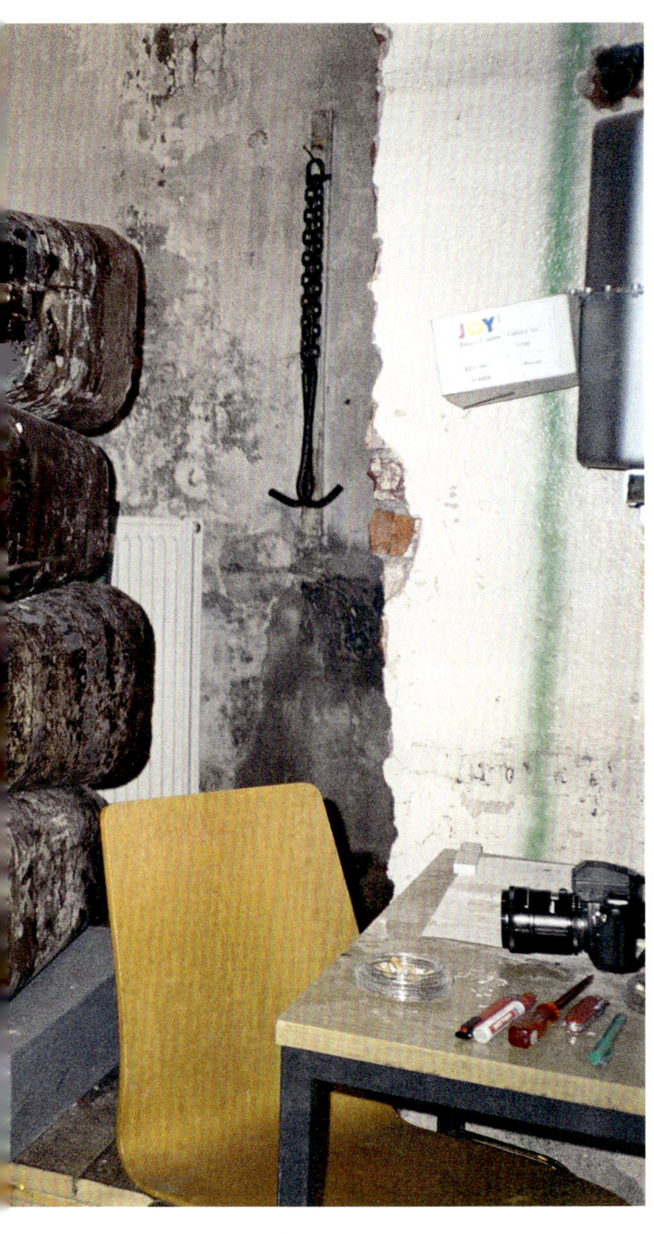

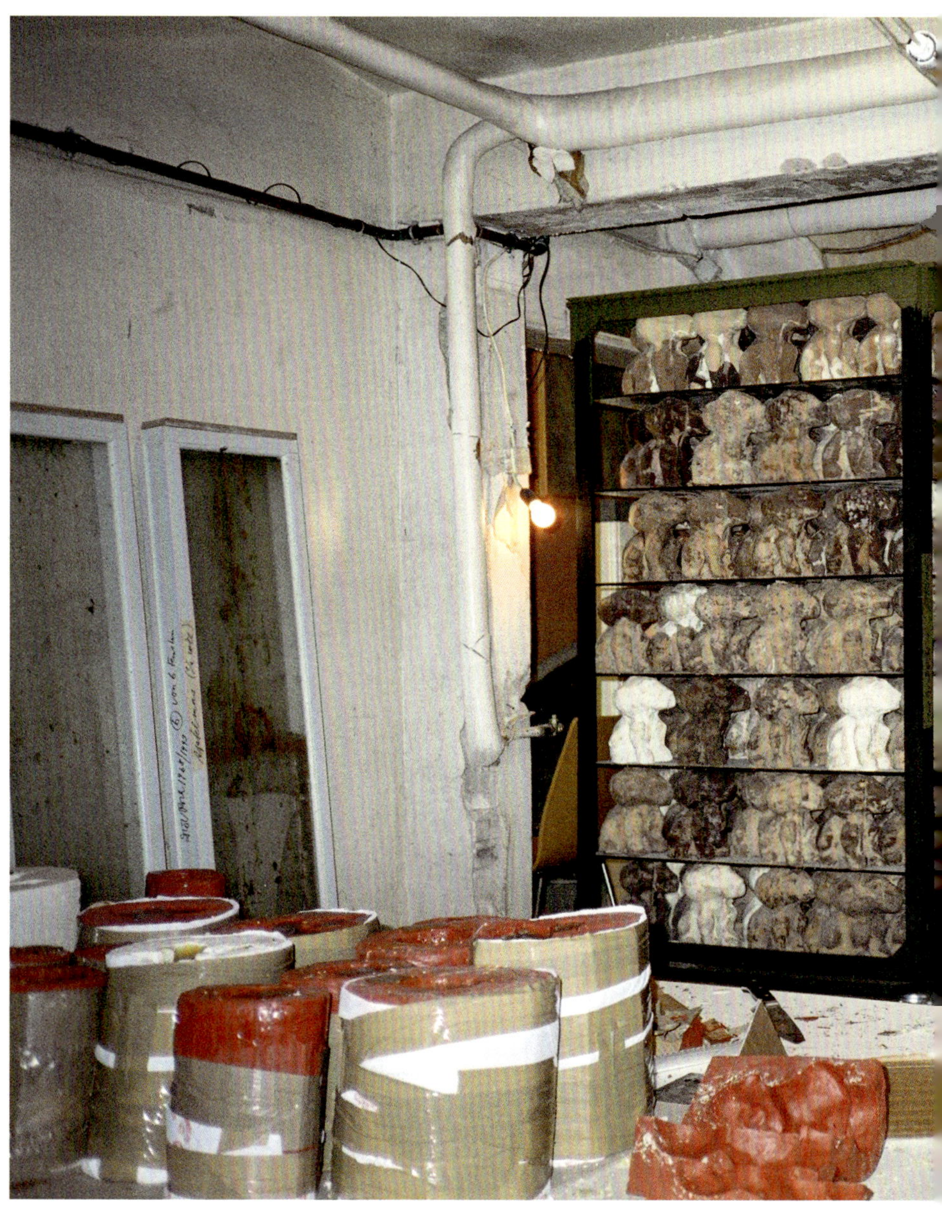

Silikon-Gussformen für die Figuren (vorne) und Hohlform für die *Coquillen-Zwerge* (rechts).
Silicon casts for the figures (at the front) and hollow form for the *Coquille Gnomes* (on the right).

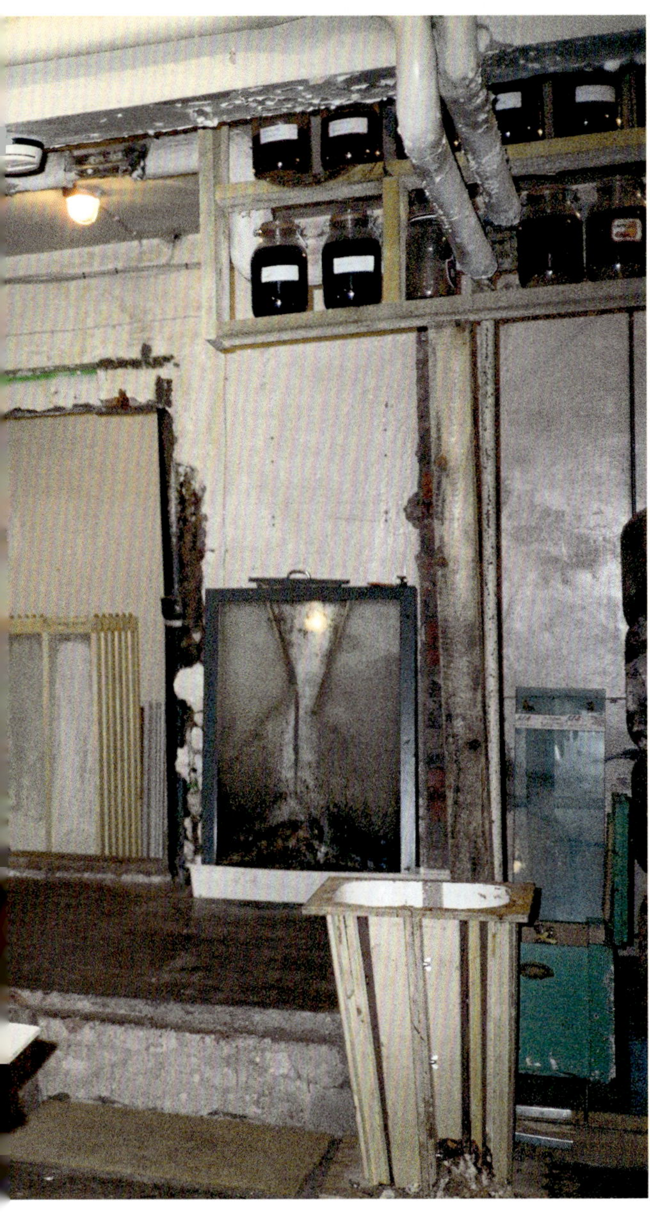

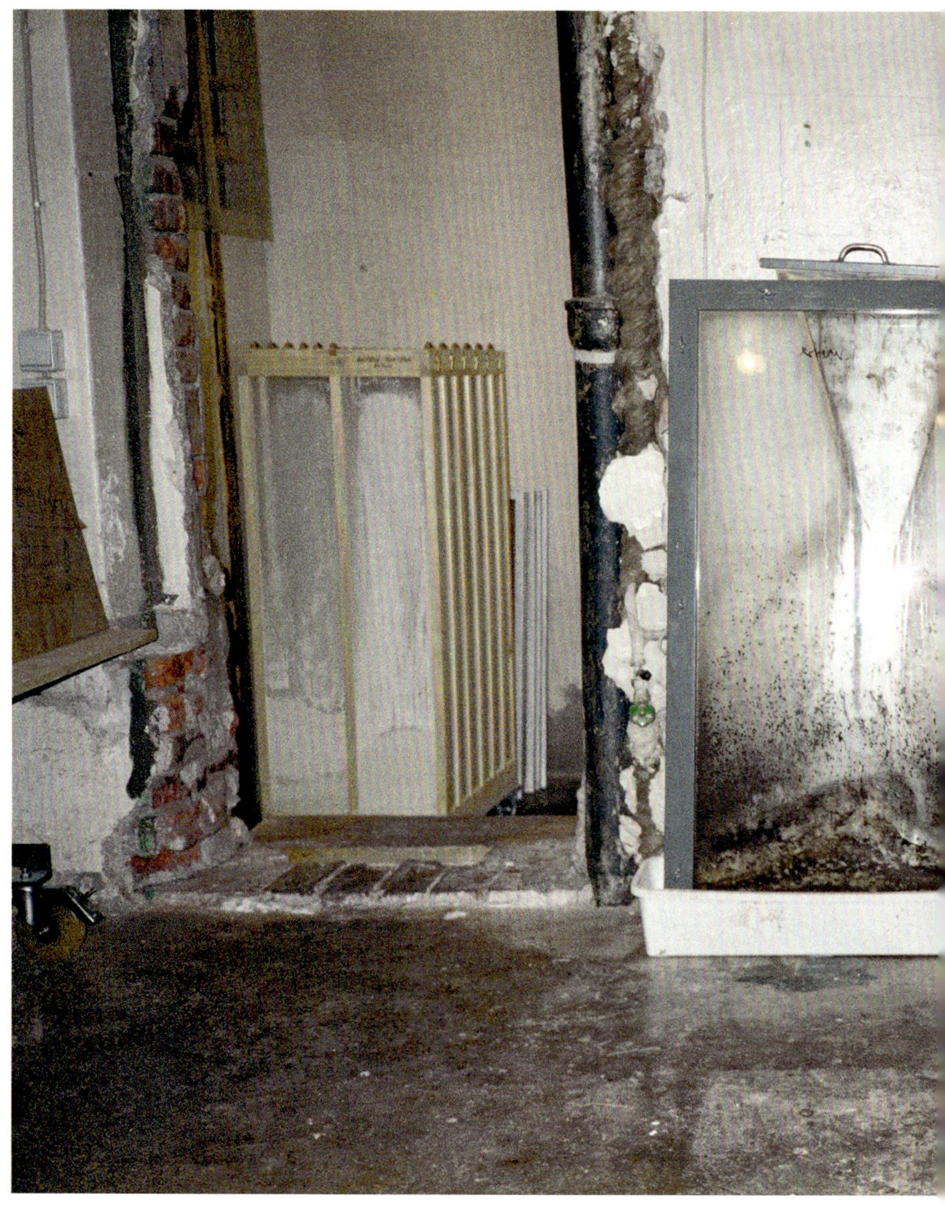

Flacher Behälter, Dosengemüse in beidseitig verglastem Holzrahmen mit Einfülltrichter.
Flat Container, tinned vegetables in wooden frame glazed on both sides with filling funnel.

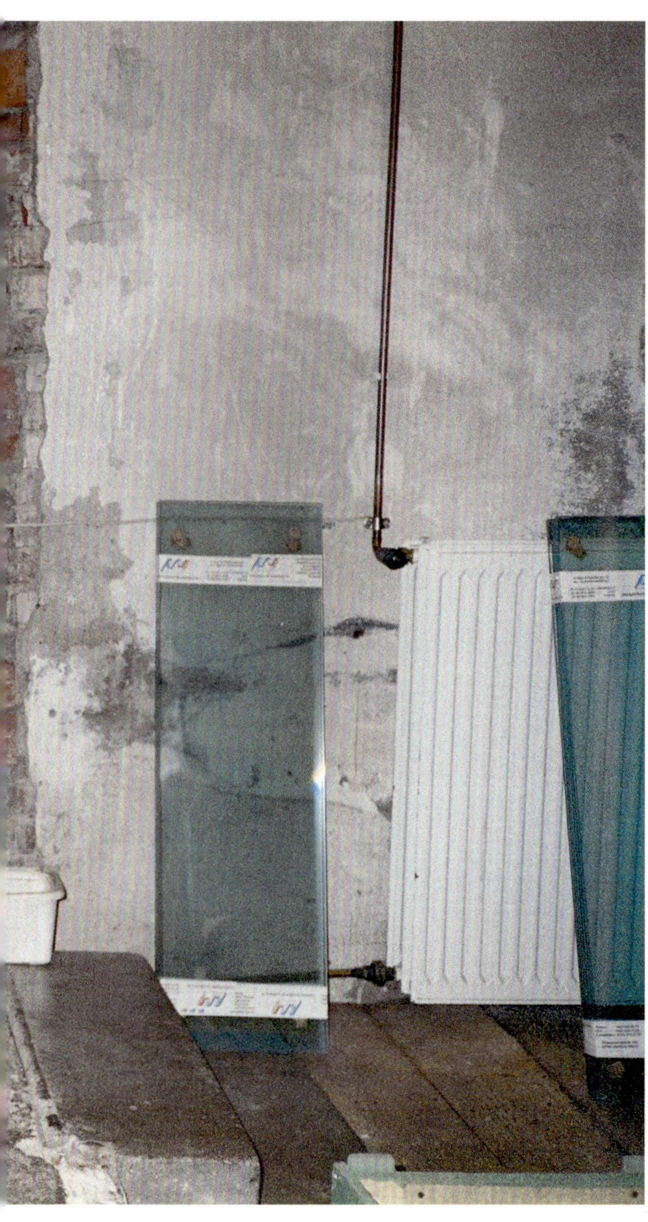

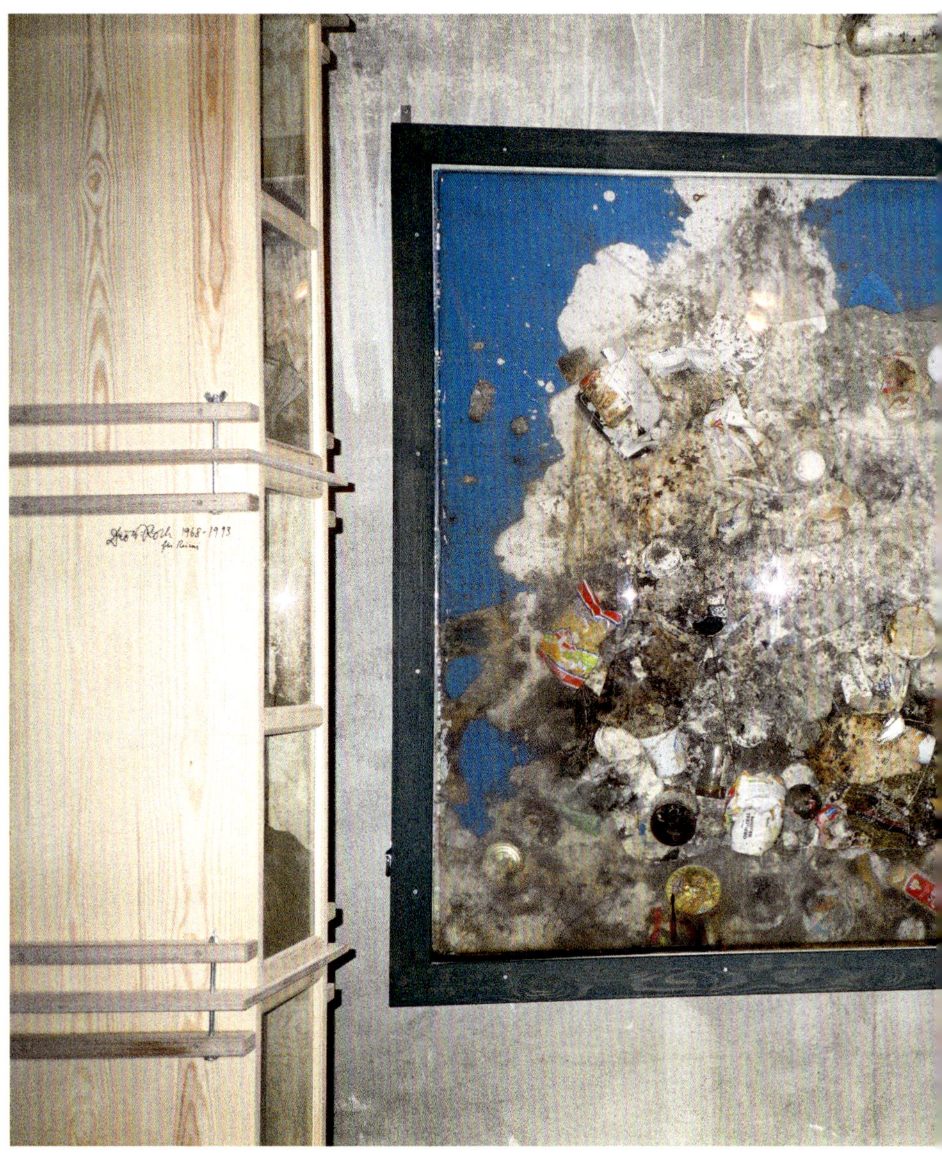

Grosse Insel Nr. 2, Haufen aus organischen Materialien, Abfall, Gips, Draht, Schrauben, Nägel, Acrylfarbe.
Large Island no 2, heap of organic materials, refuse, plaster, wire, screws, nails, acrylic paint.

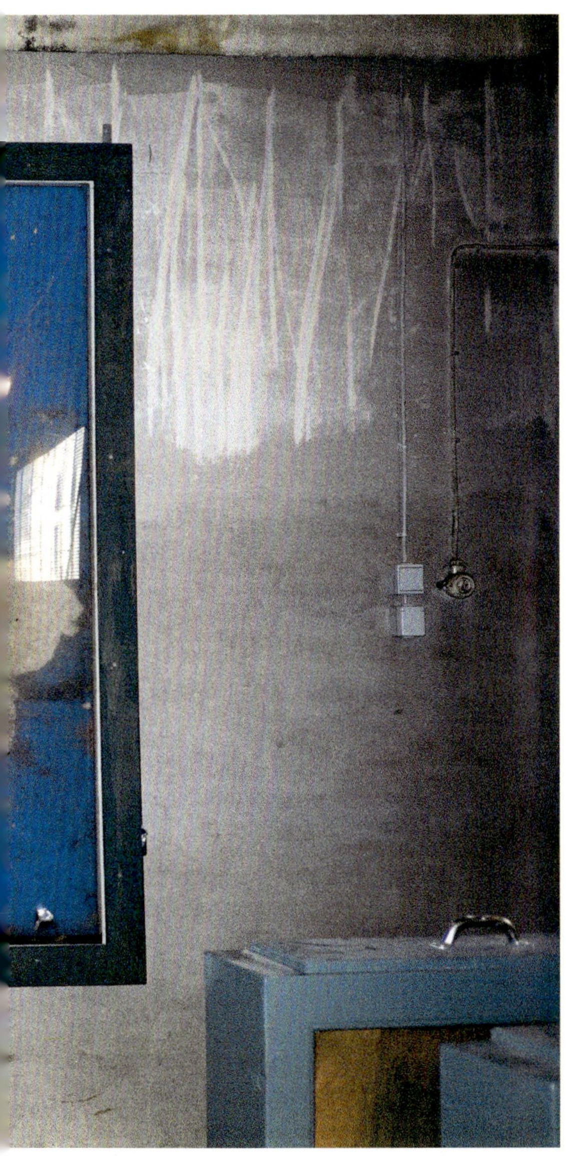

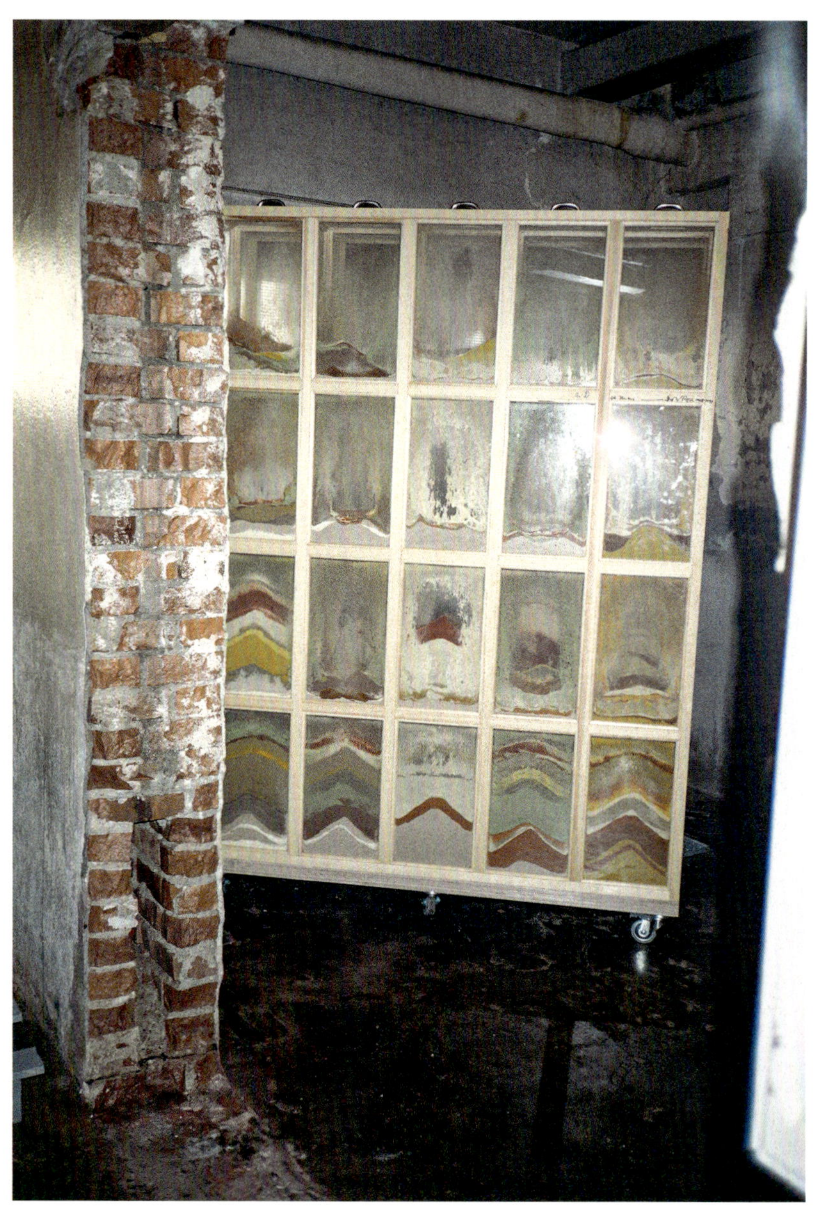

Gewürzkubikel, verschiedene Gewürze.
Spice Cubicle, different spices.

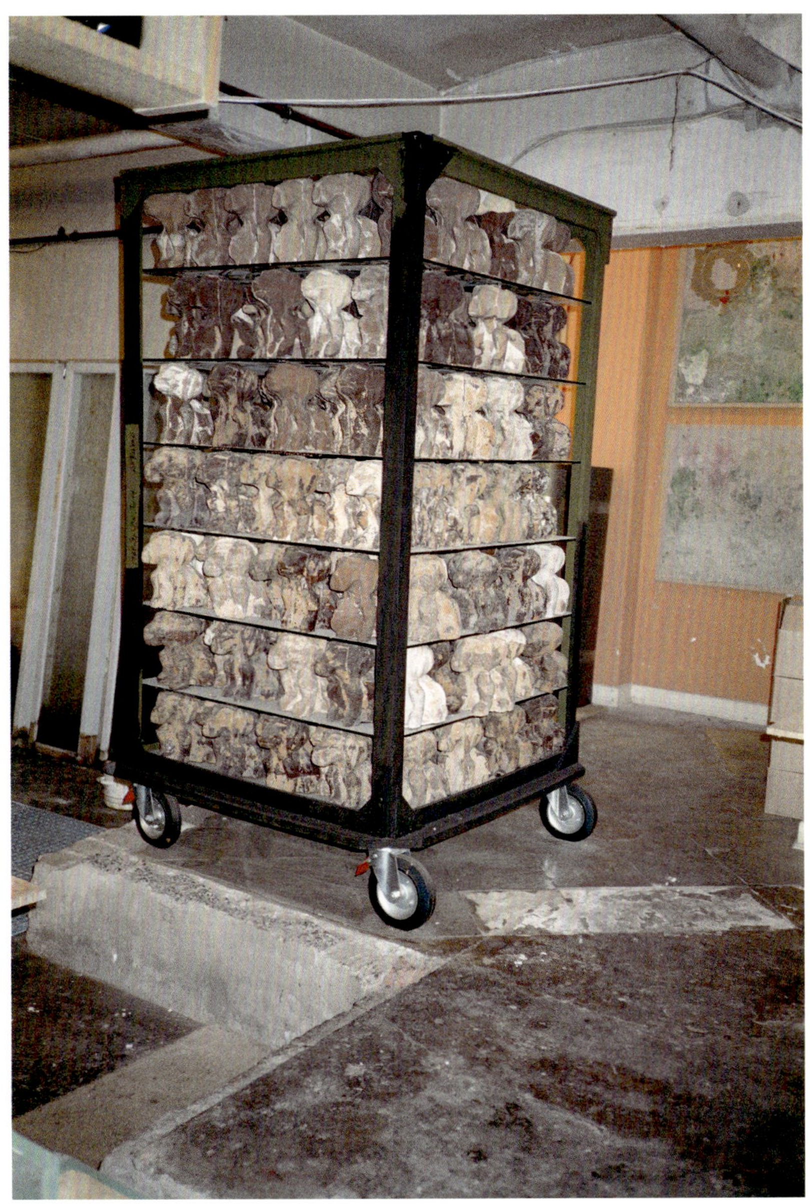

Löwenturm mit Gussfiguren *Selbstlöwe,* Schokolade.
Lion Tower with cast figures *Self Lion,* chocolate.

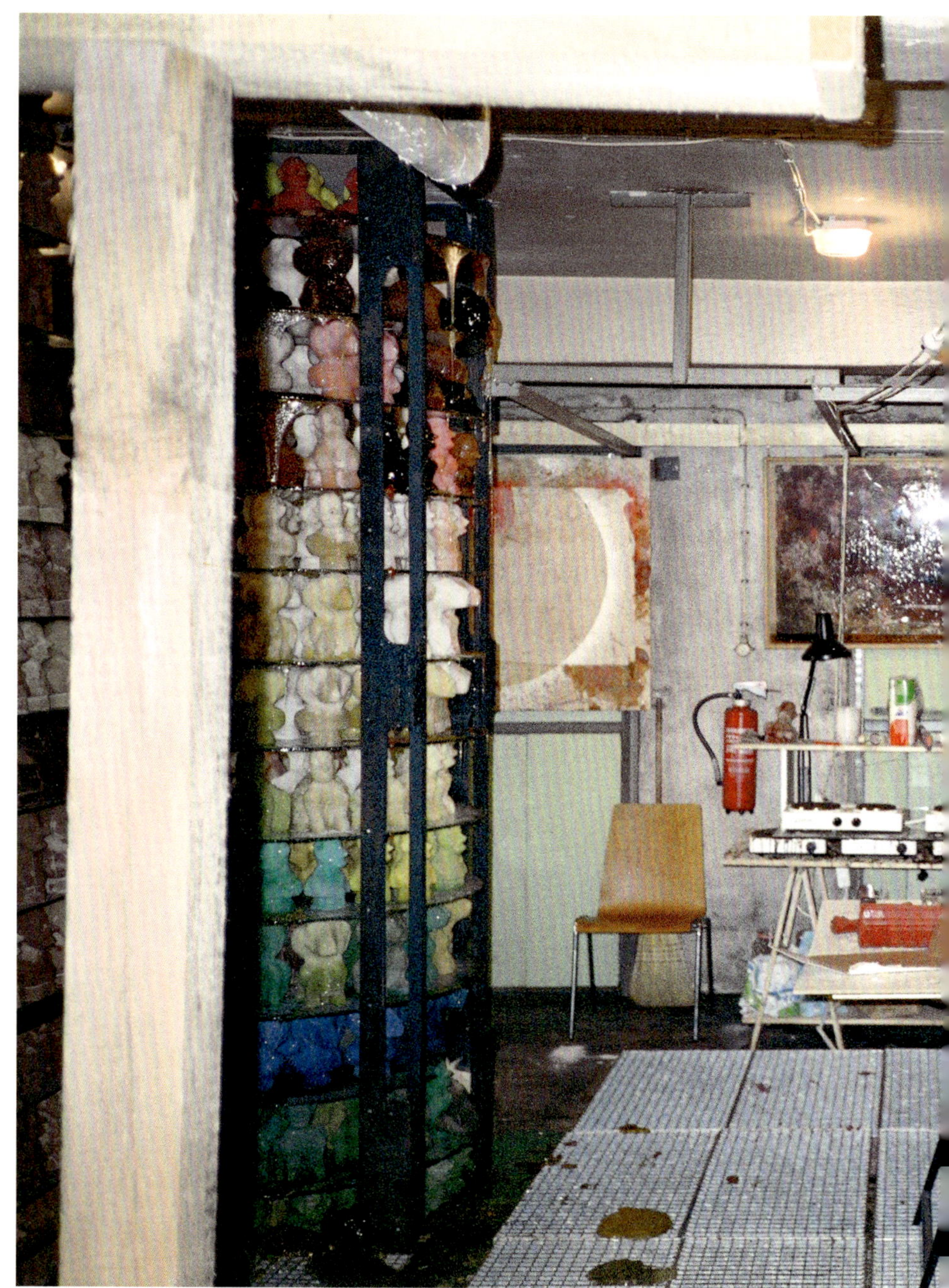

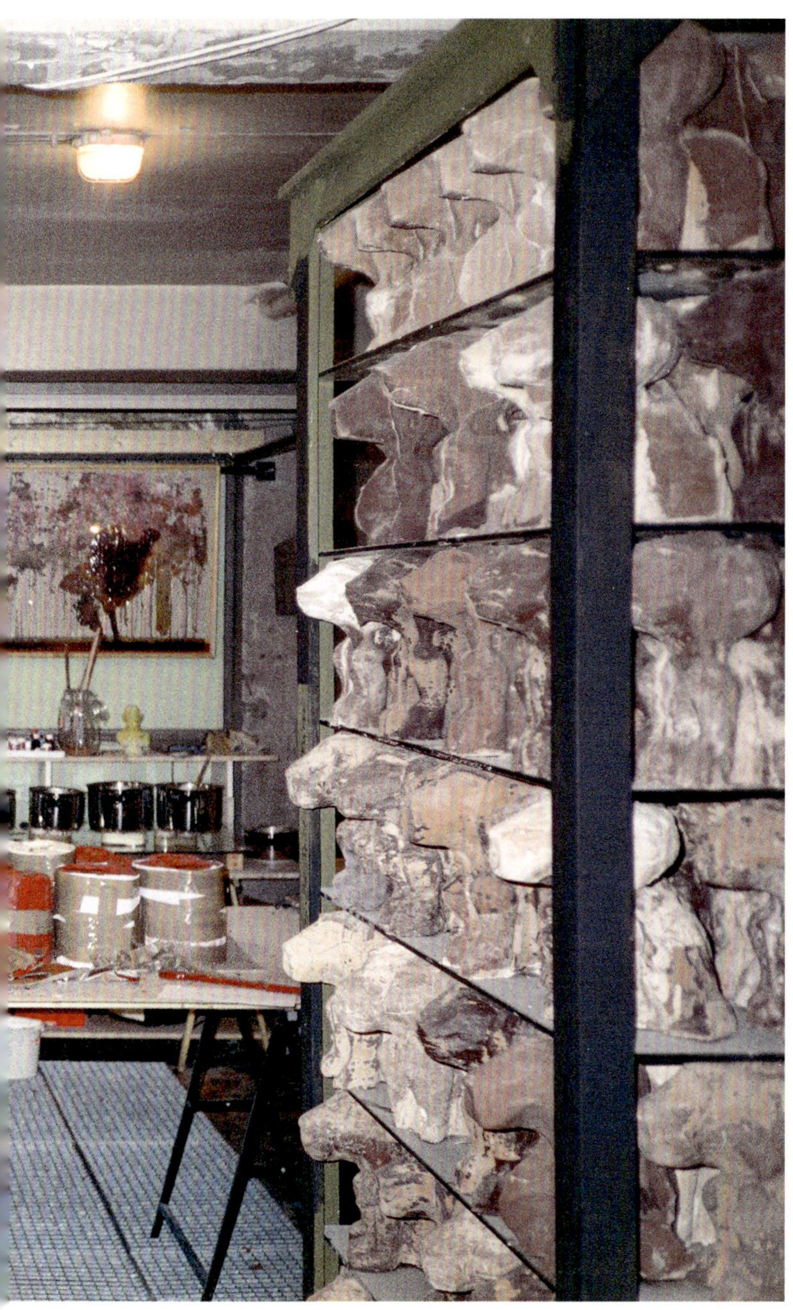

Selbstturm mit Gussfiguren *Selbstbildnis als alter Mann,* Schokolade. *Zuckerturm* mit Gussfiguren *Selbstlöwe, SelbstBüste* und *Sphinx,* Zucker, Lebensmittelfarbe, Acrylfarbe, Tinte, Tusche.
Self Tower with cast figures *Self-portrait as an Old Man,* chocolate. *Sugar Tower* with cast
figures *Self Lion, Self Bust,* and *Sphinx,* sugar, food colouring, acrylic paint, ink, Indian ink.

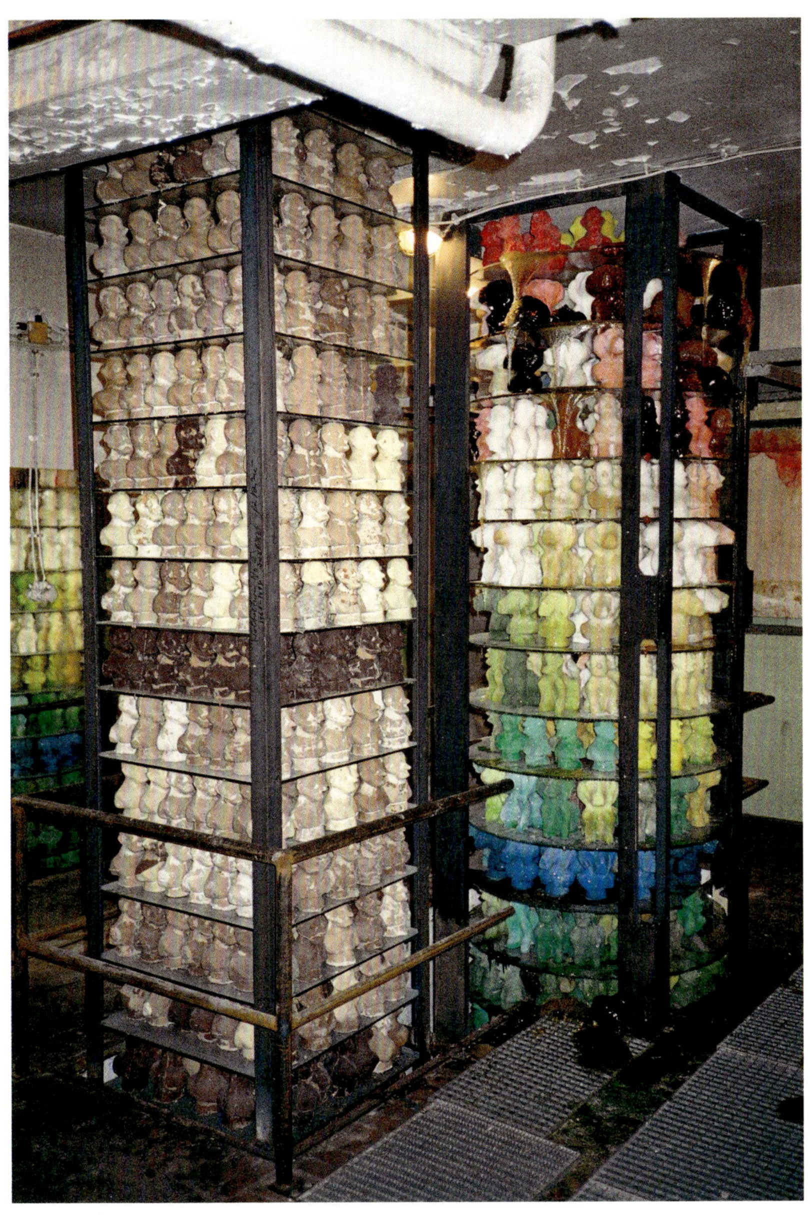

23. April 1994.
   23 April 1994.

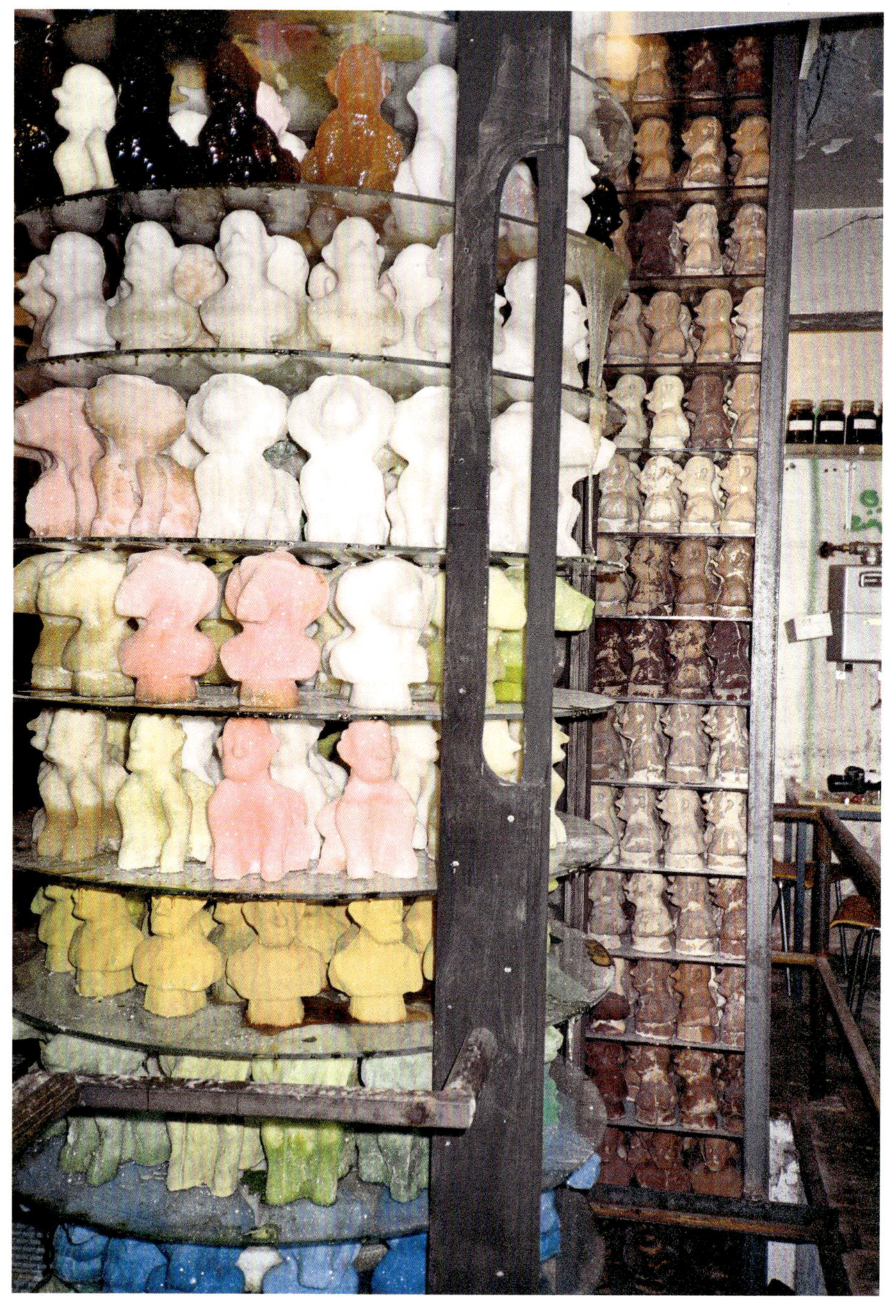

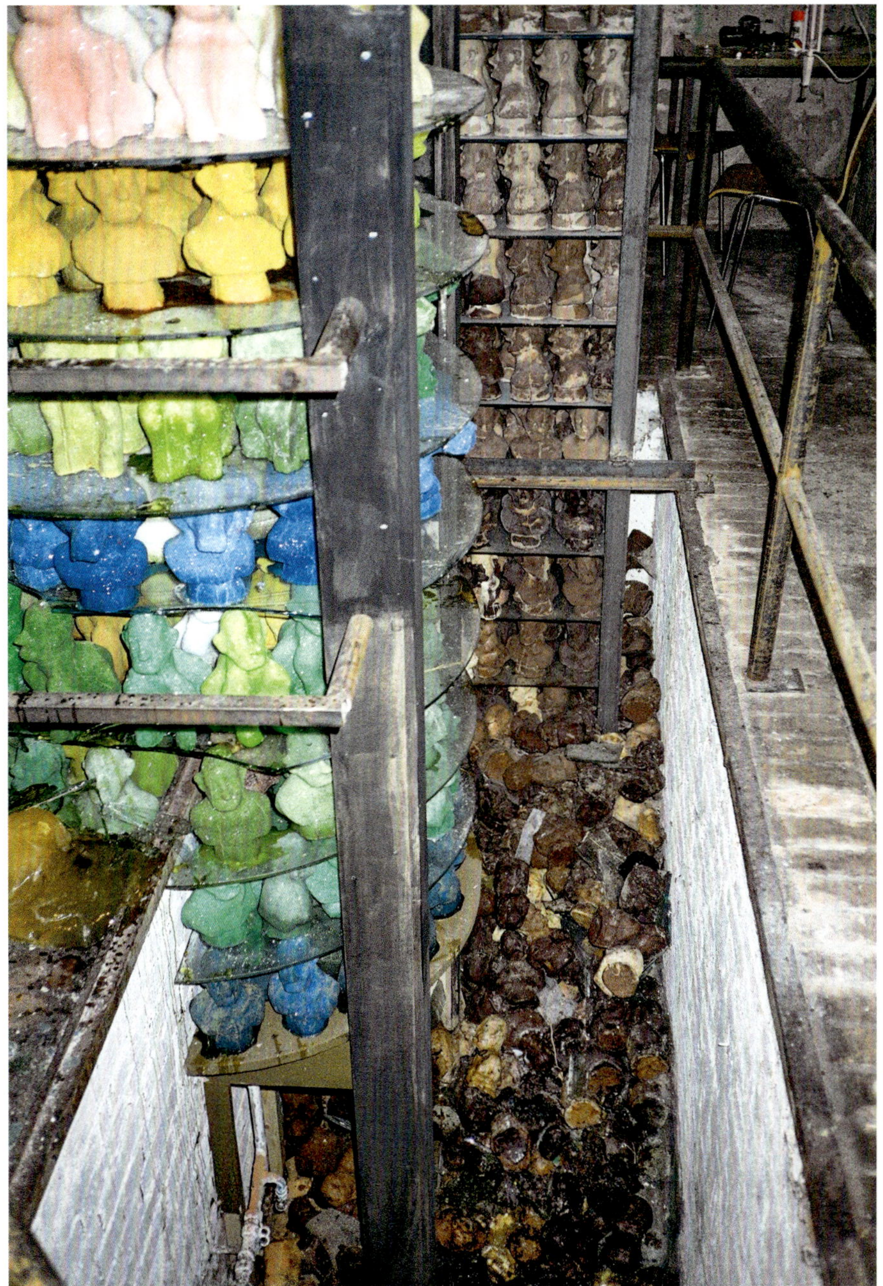

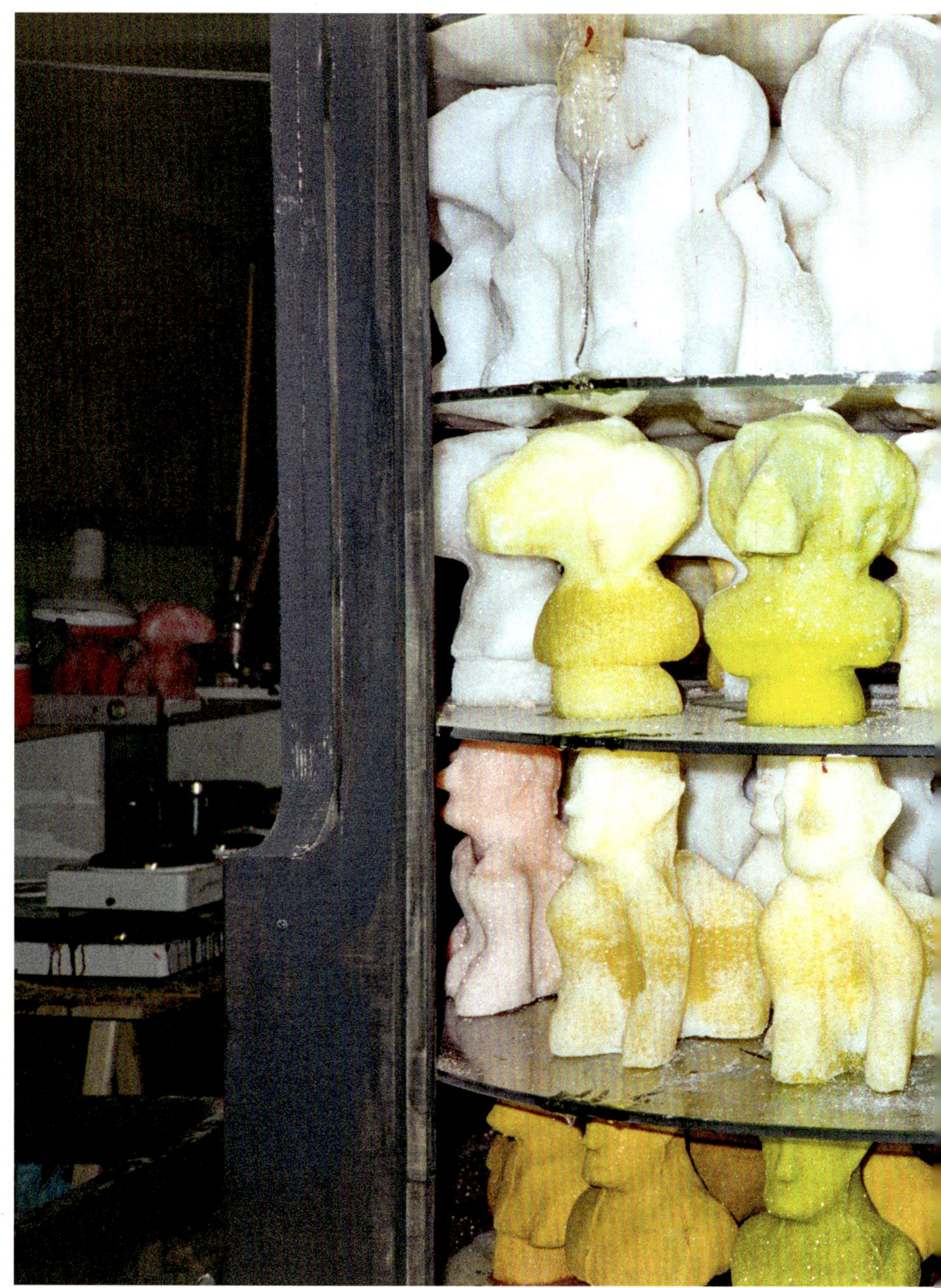

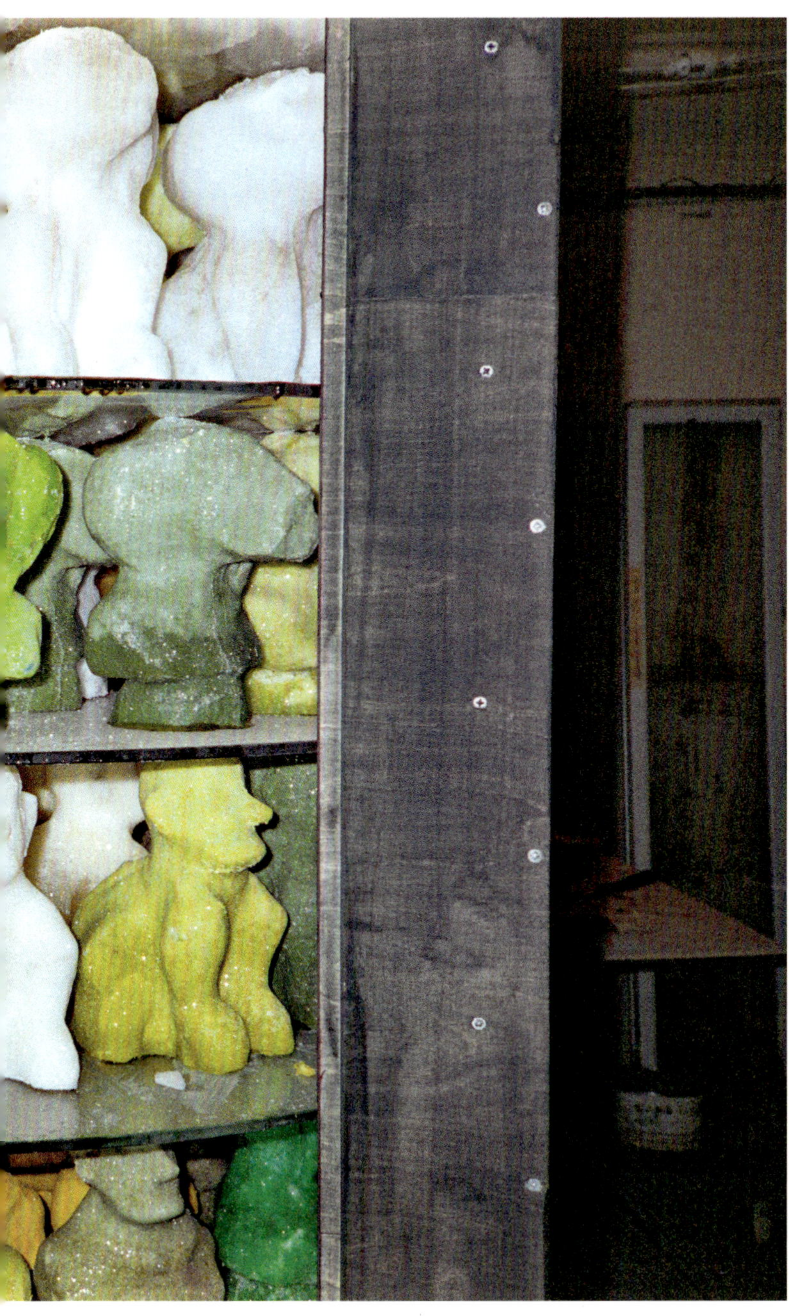

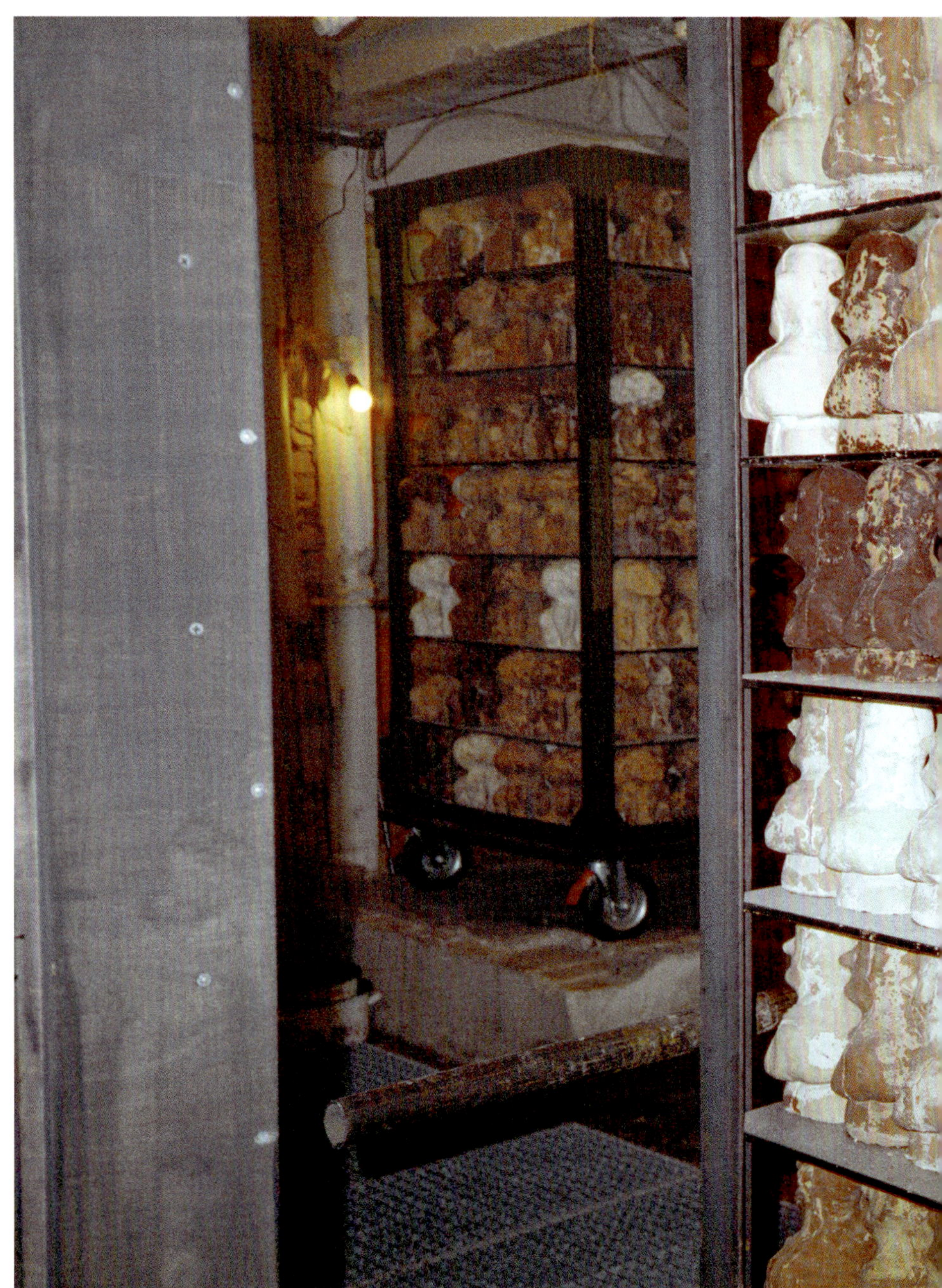

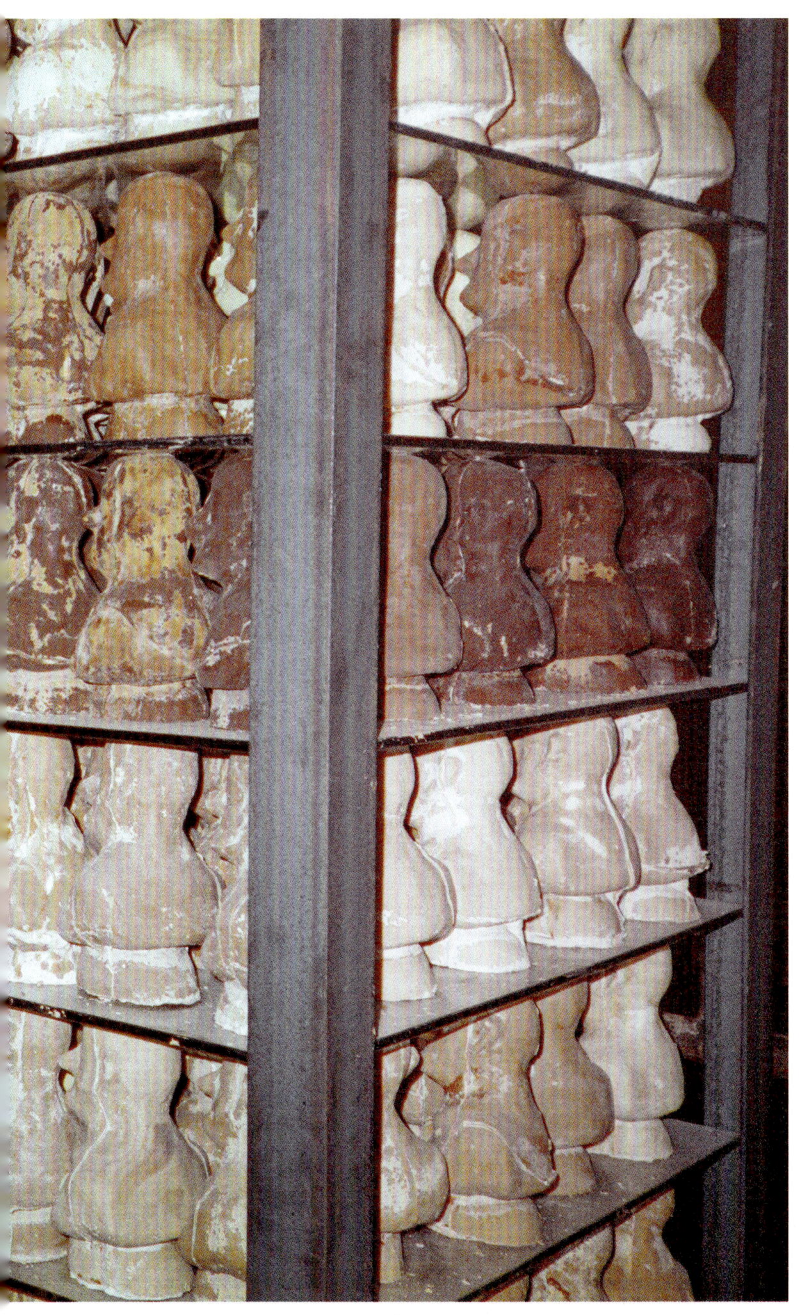

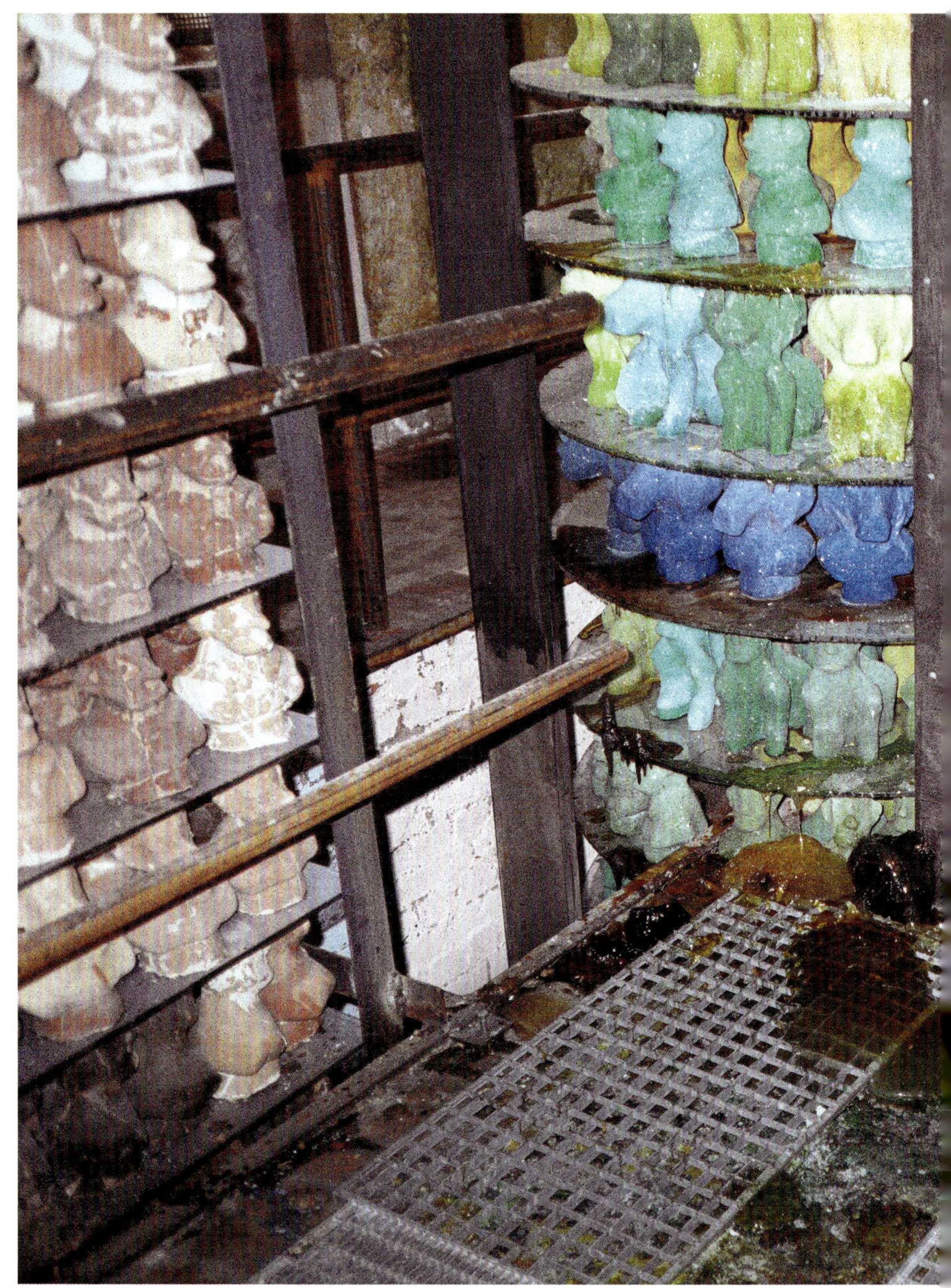

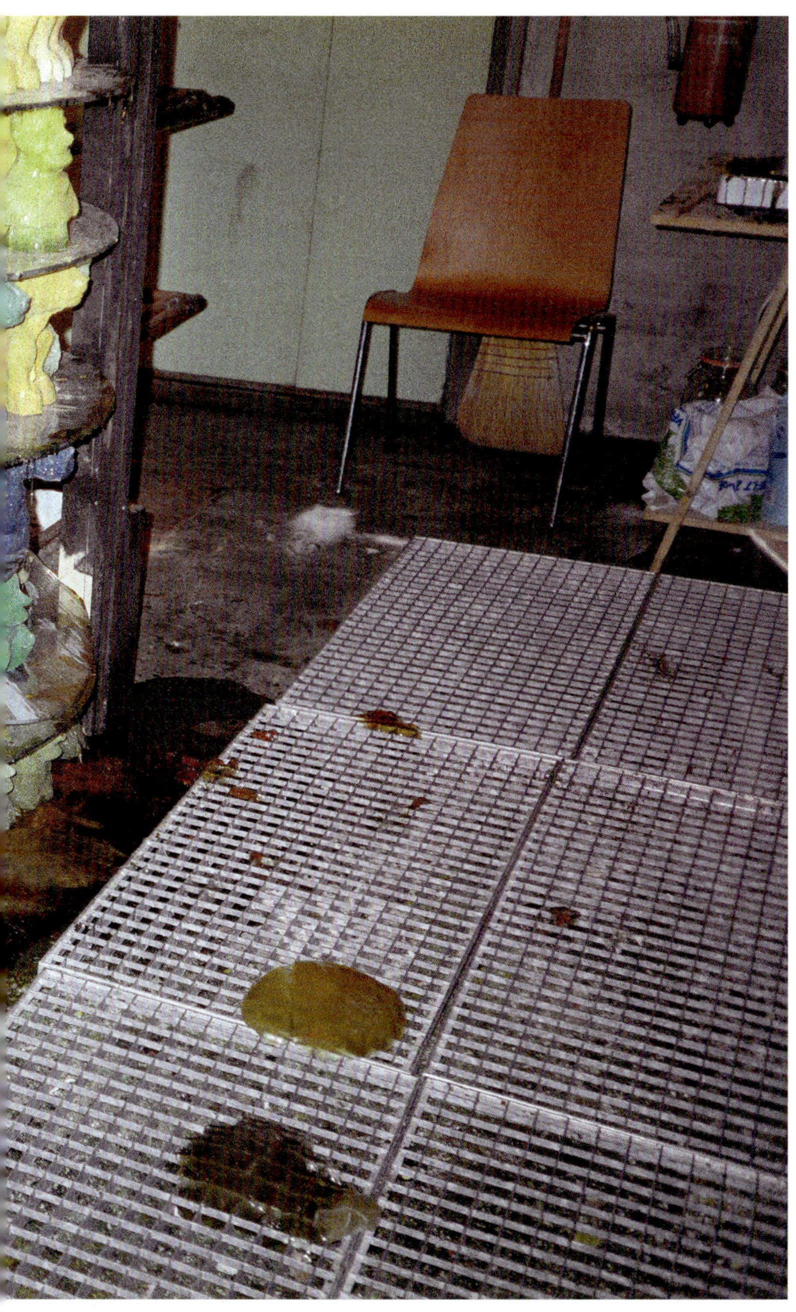

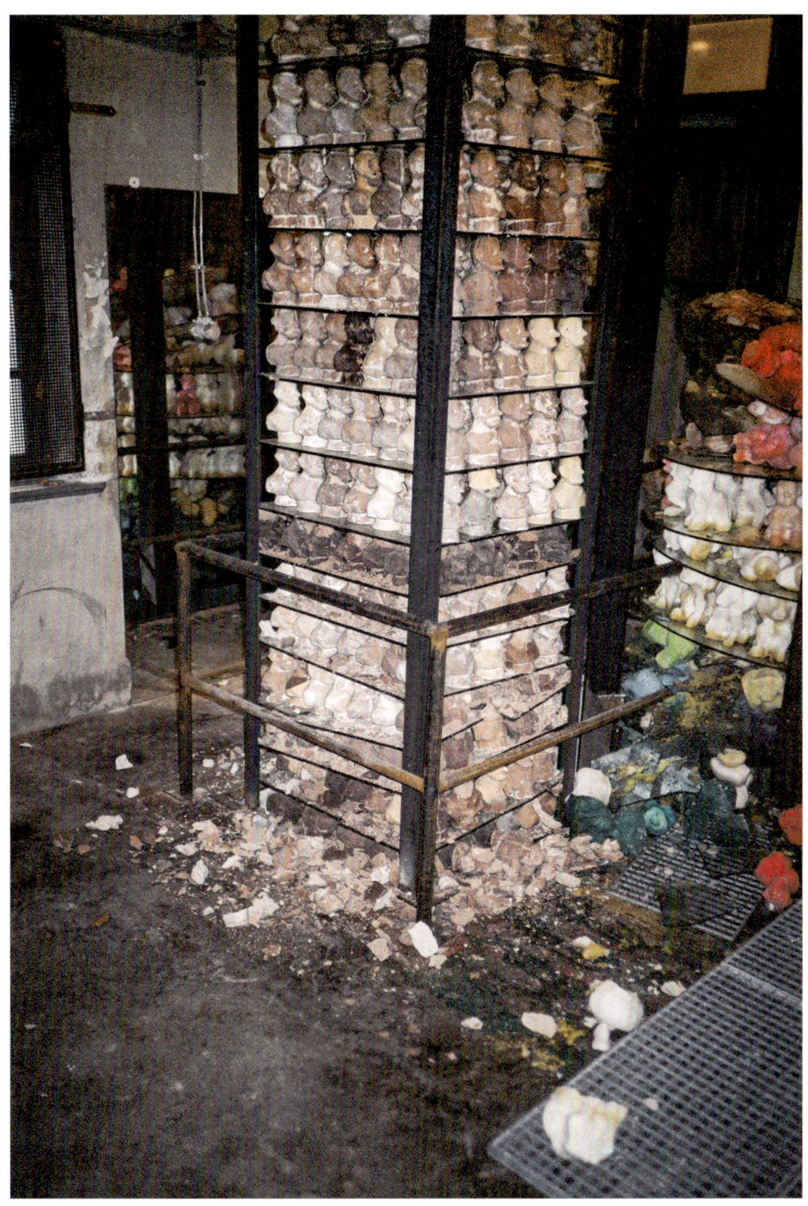

13. November 1994.
13 November 1994.

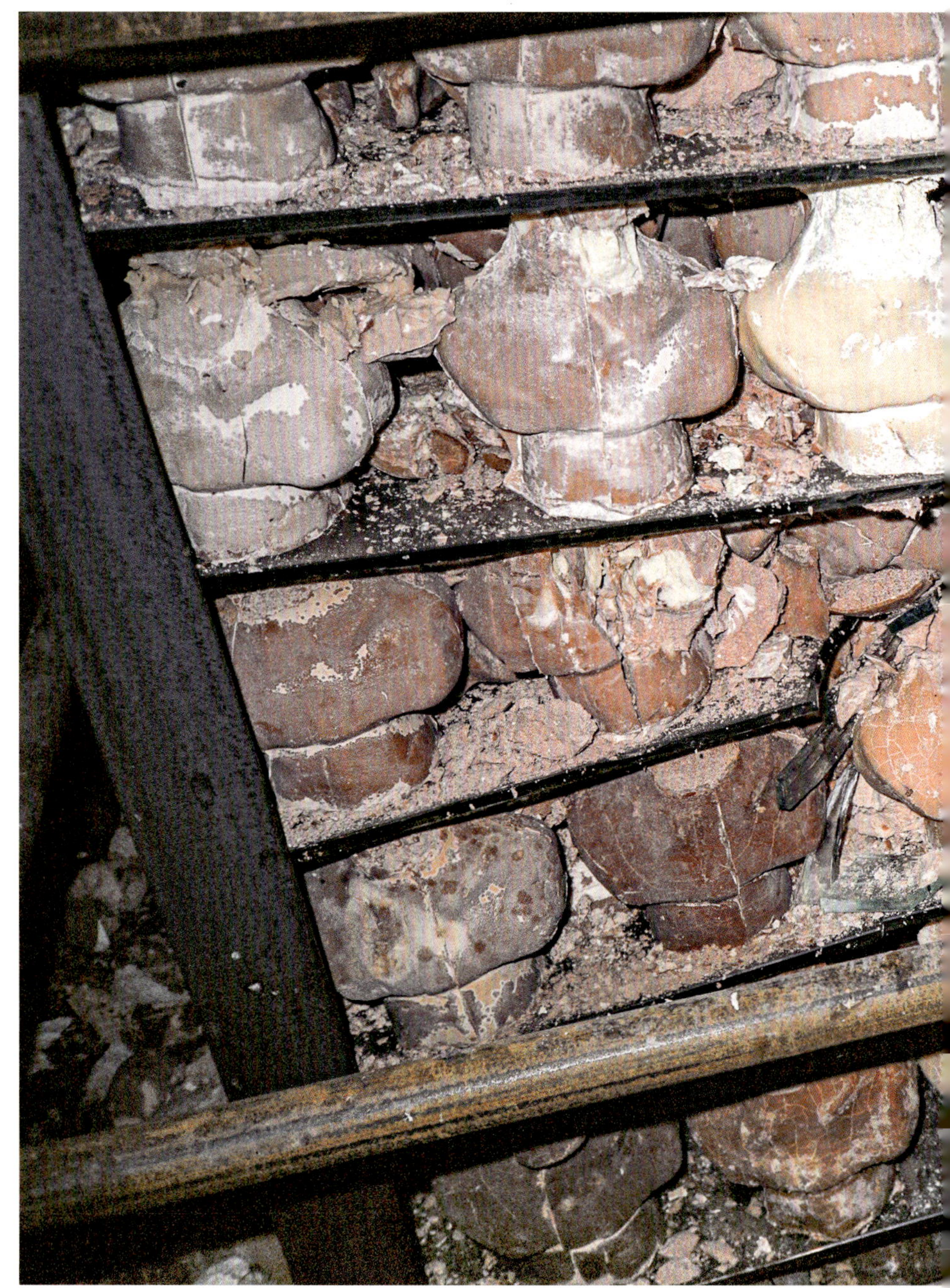

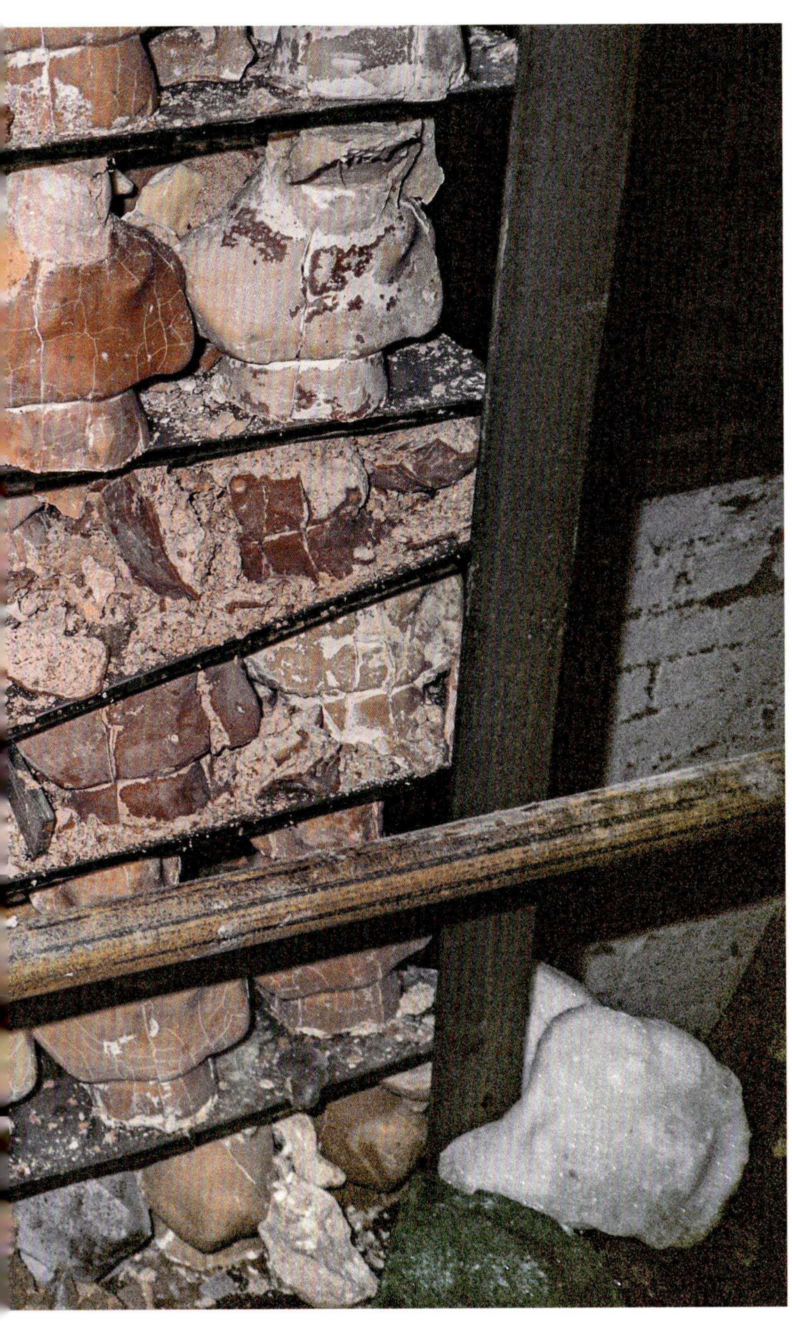

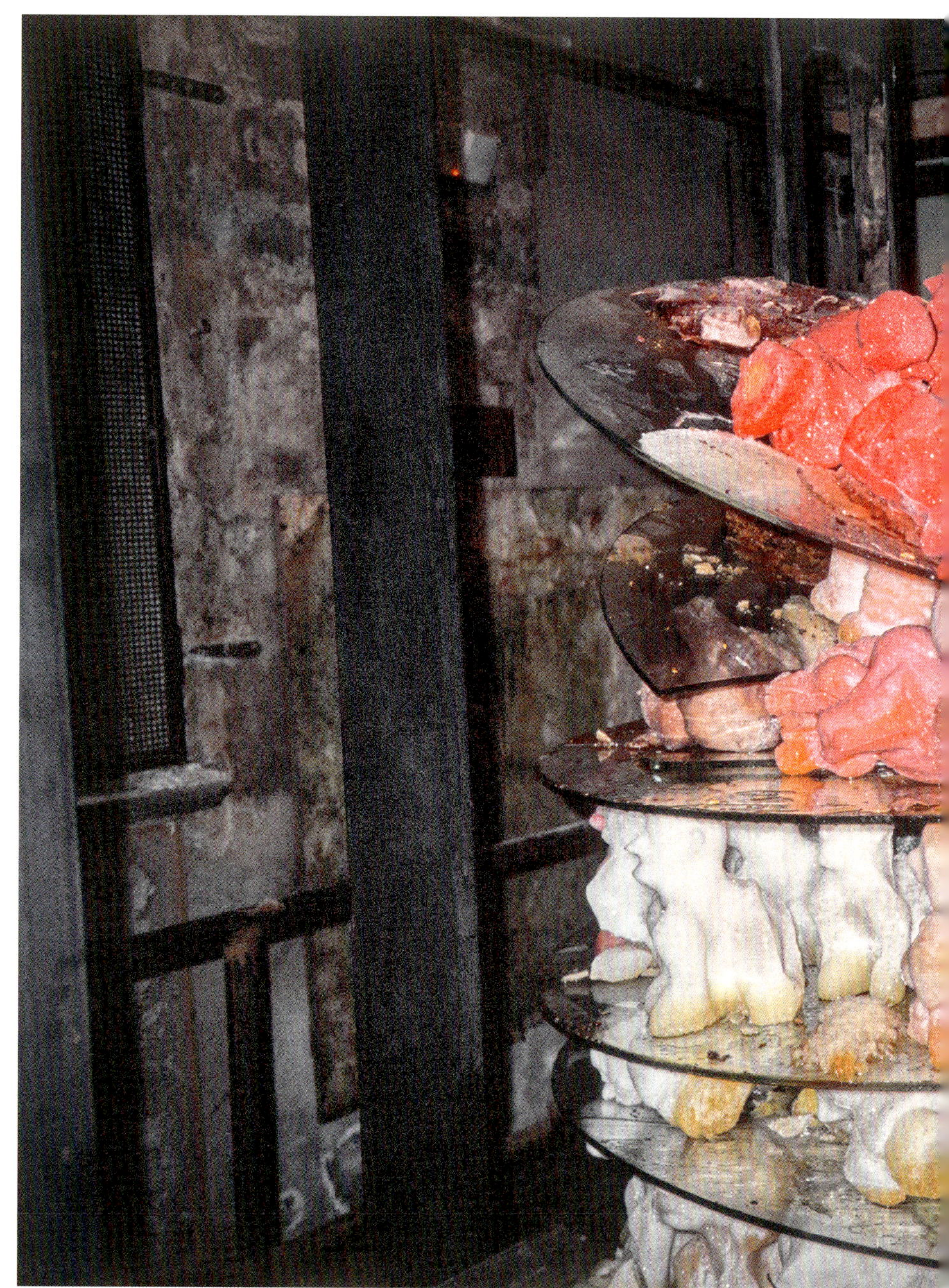

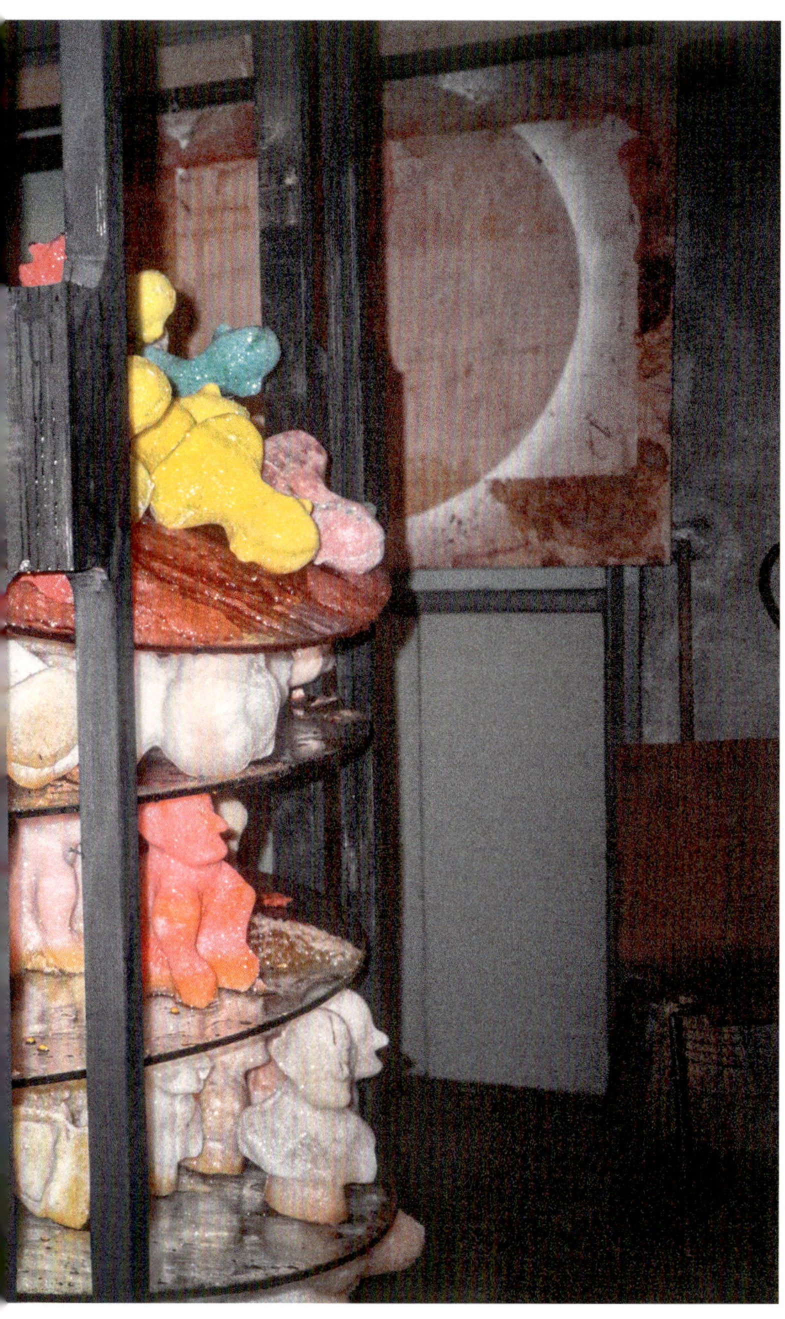

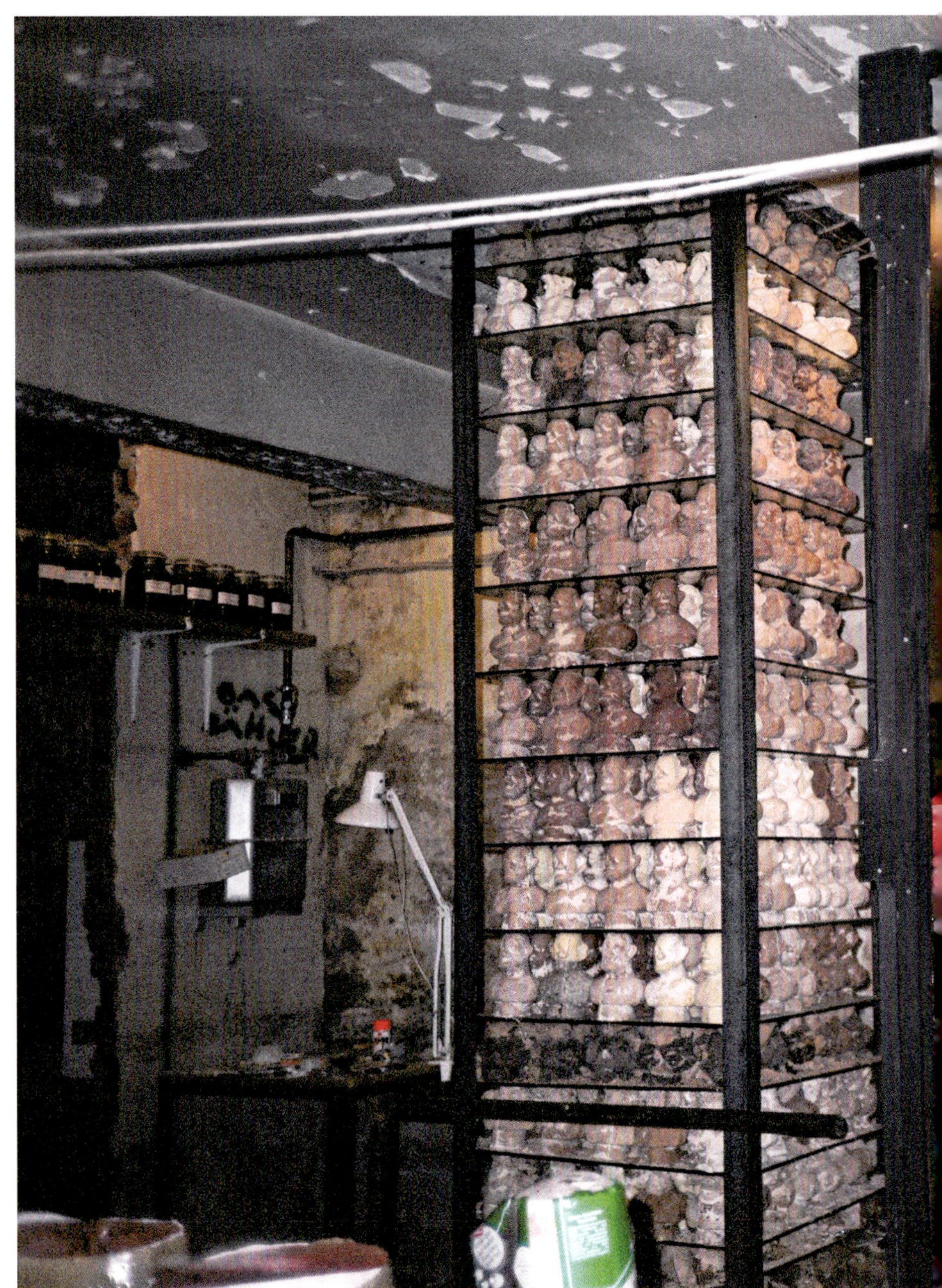

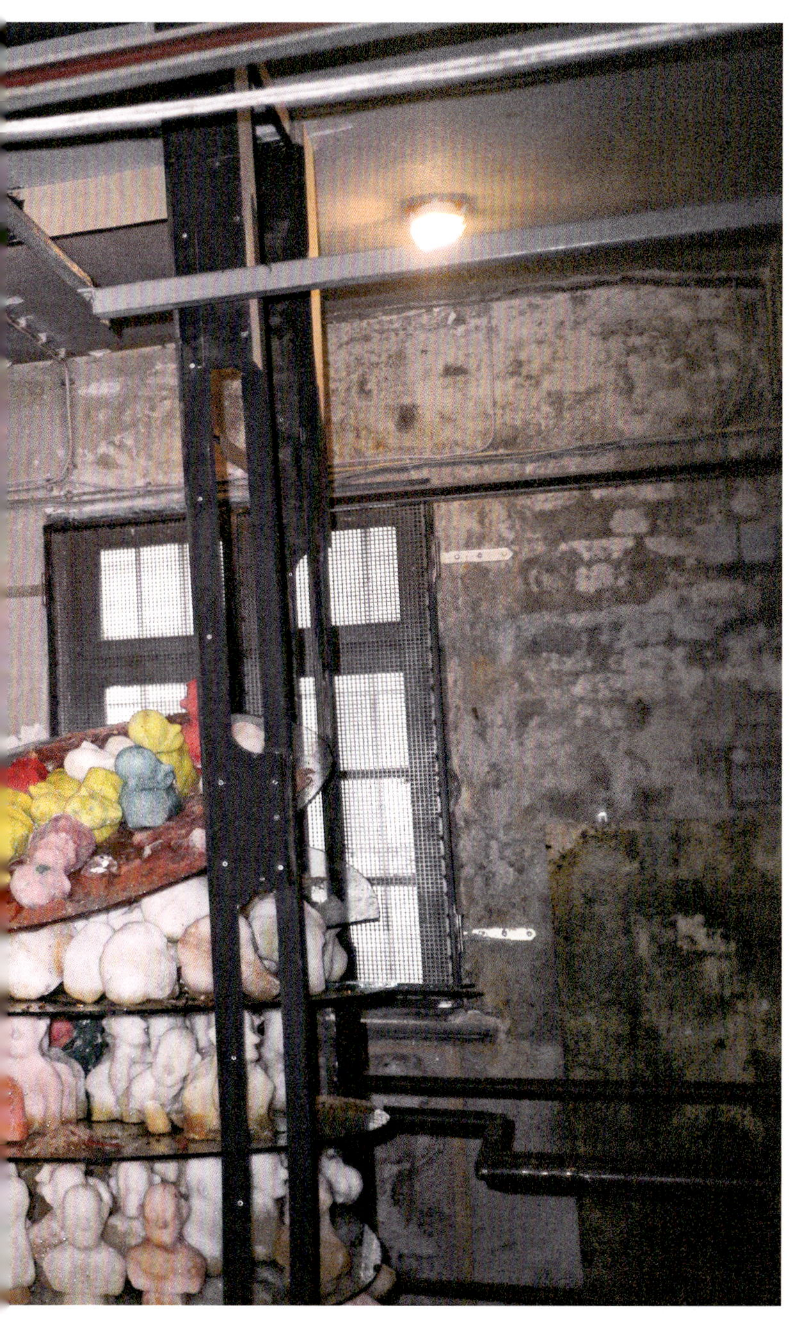

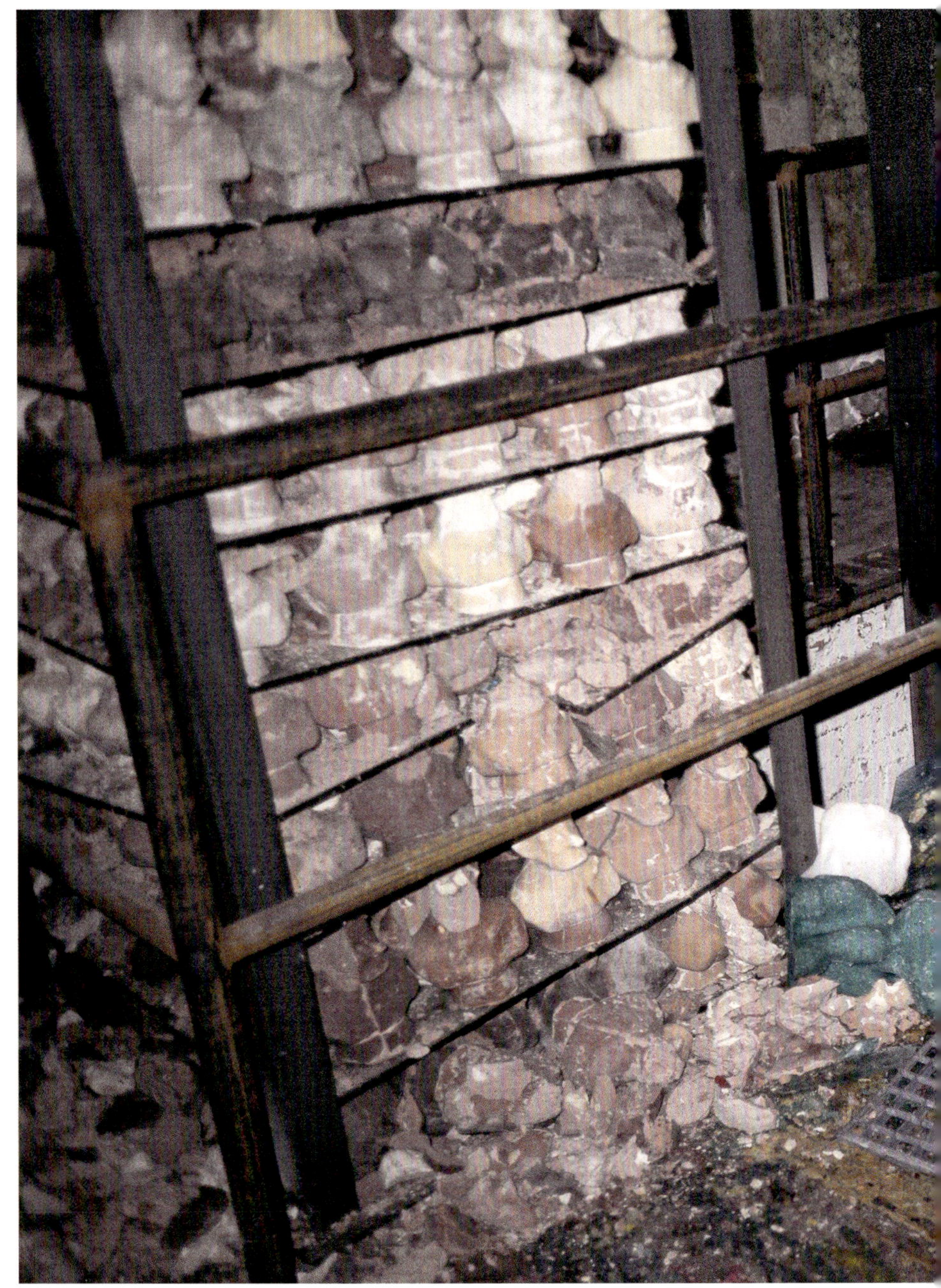

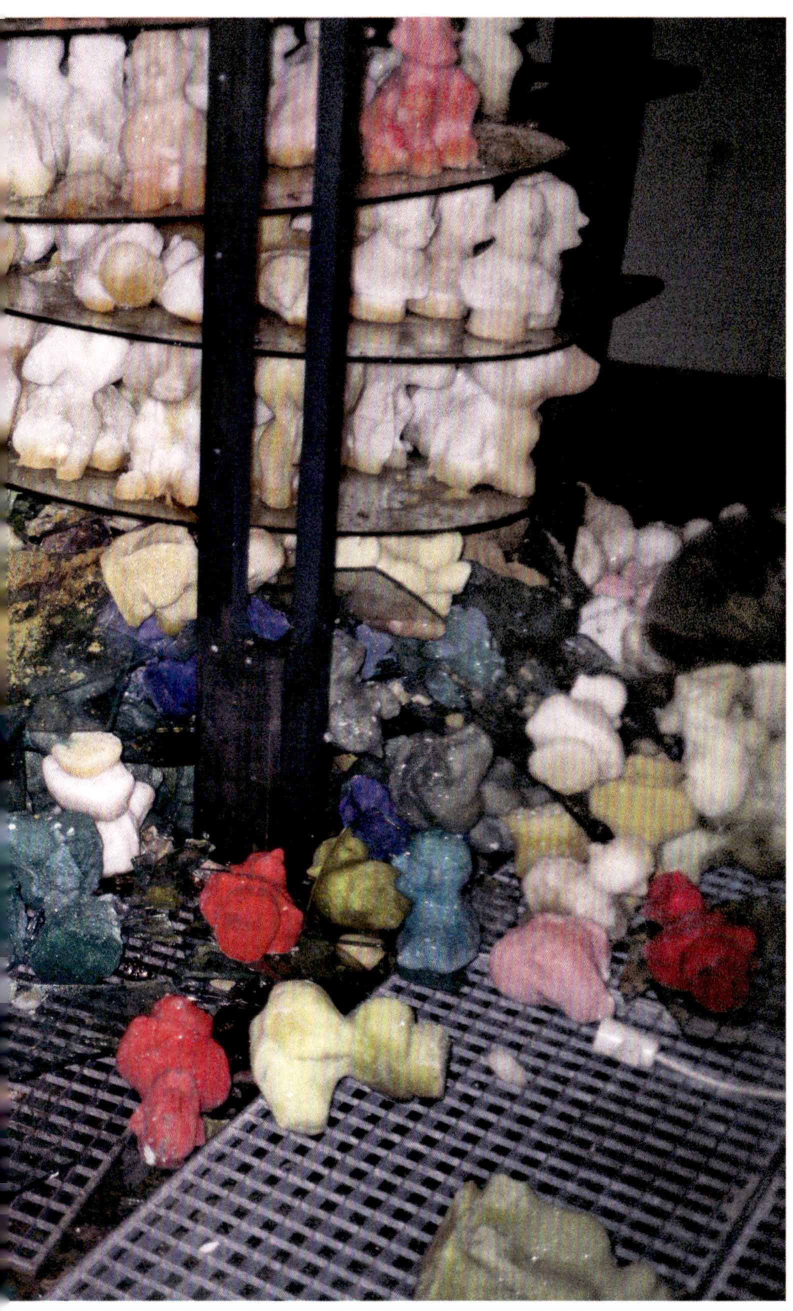

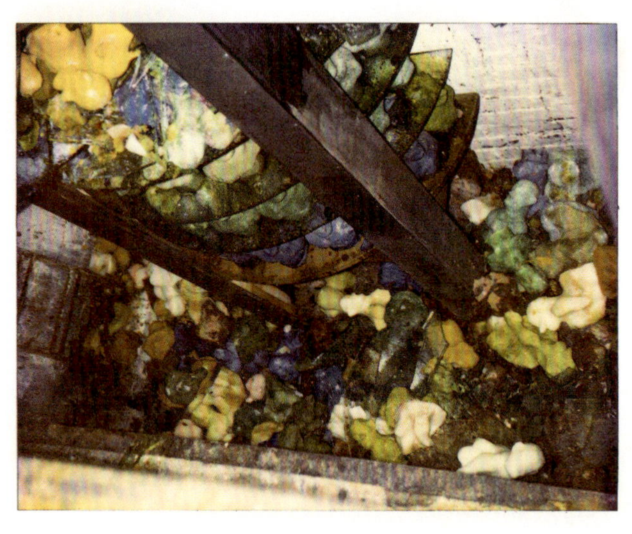

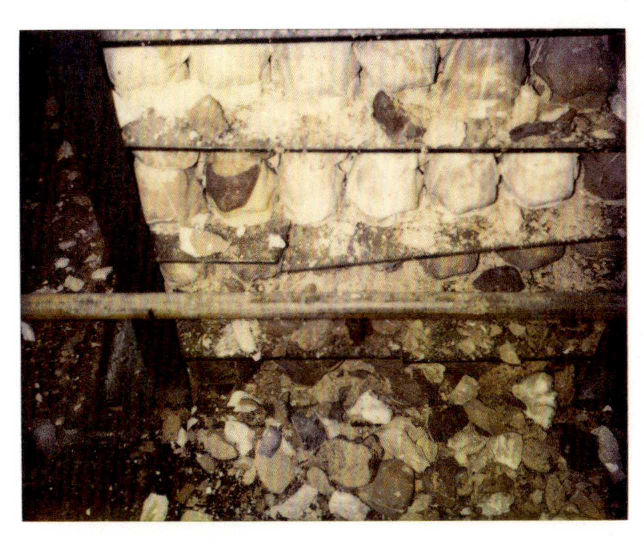

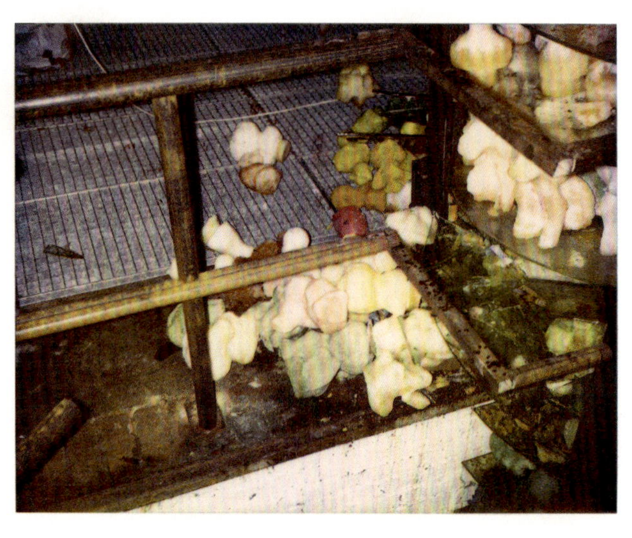

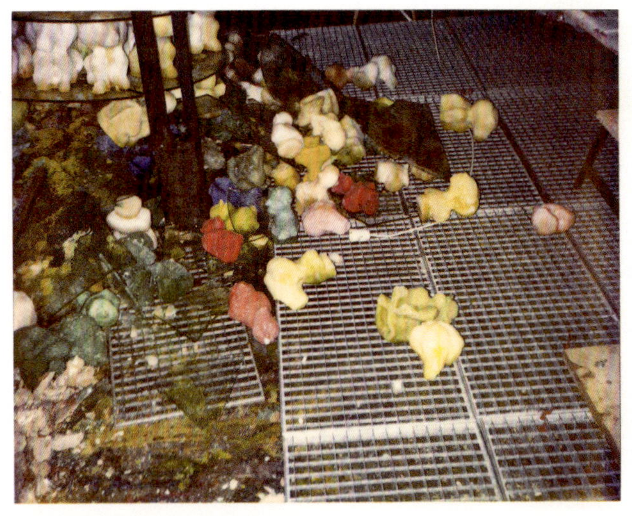

HH 13.11.94   ca. 14°°h

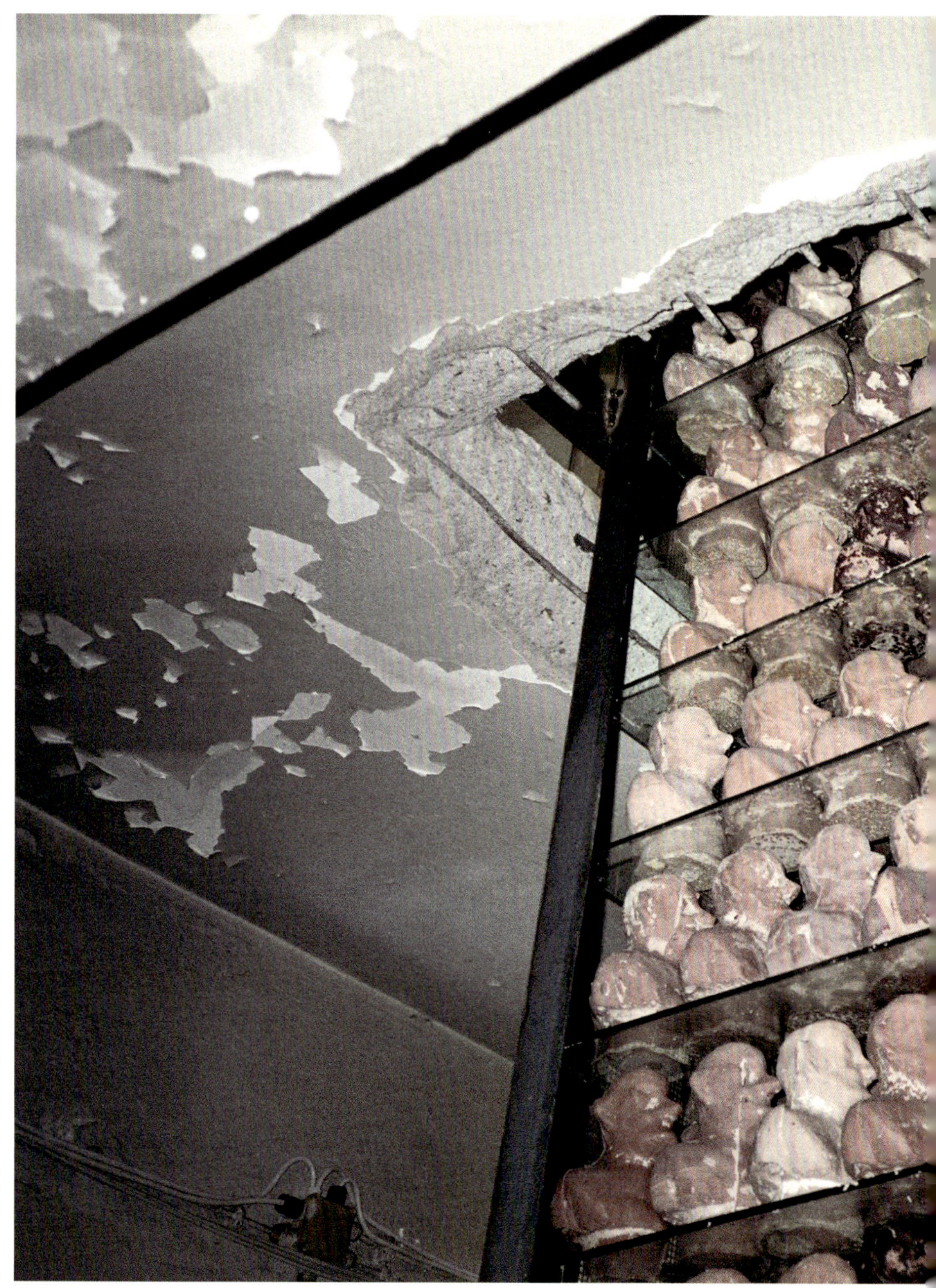

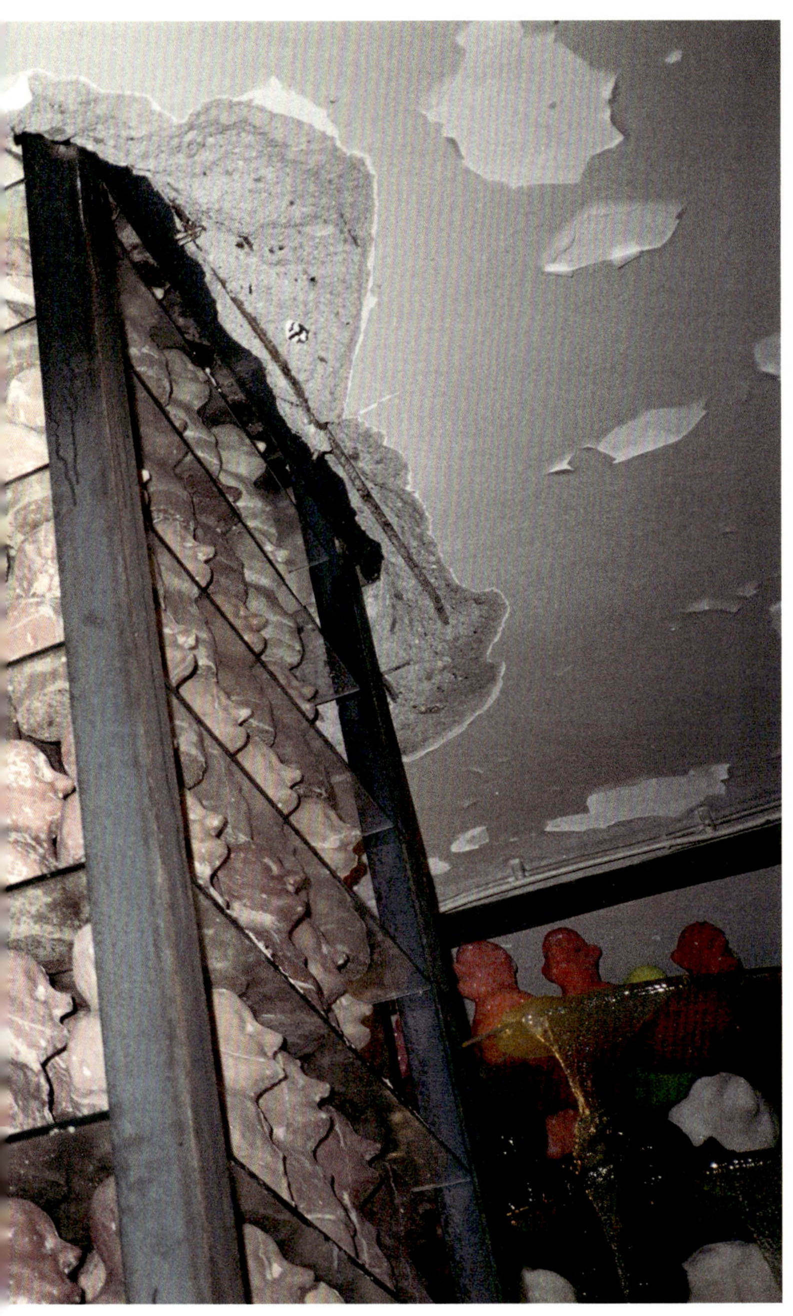

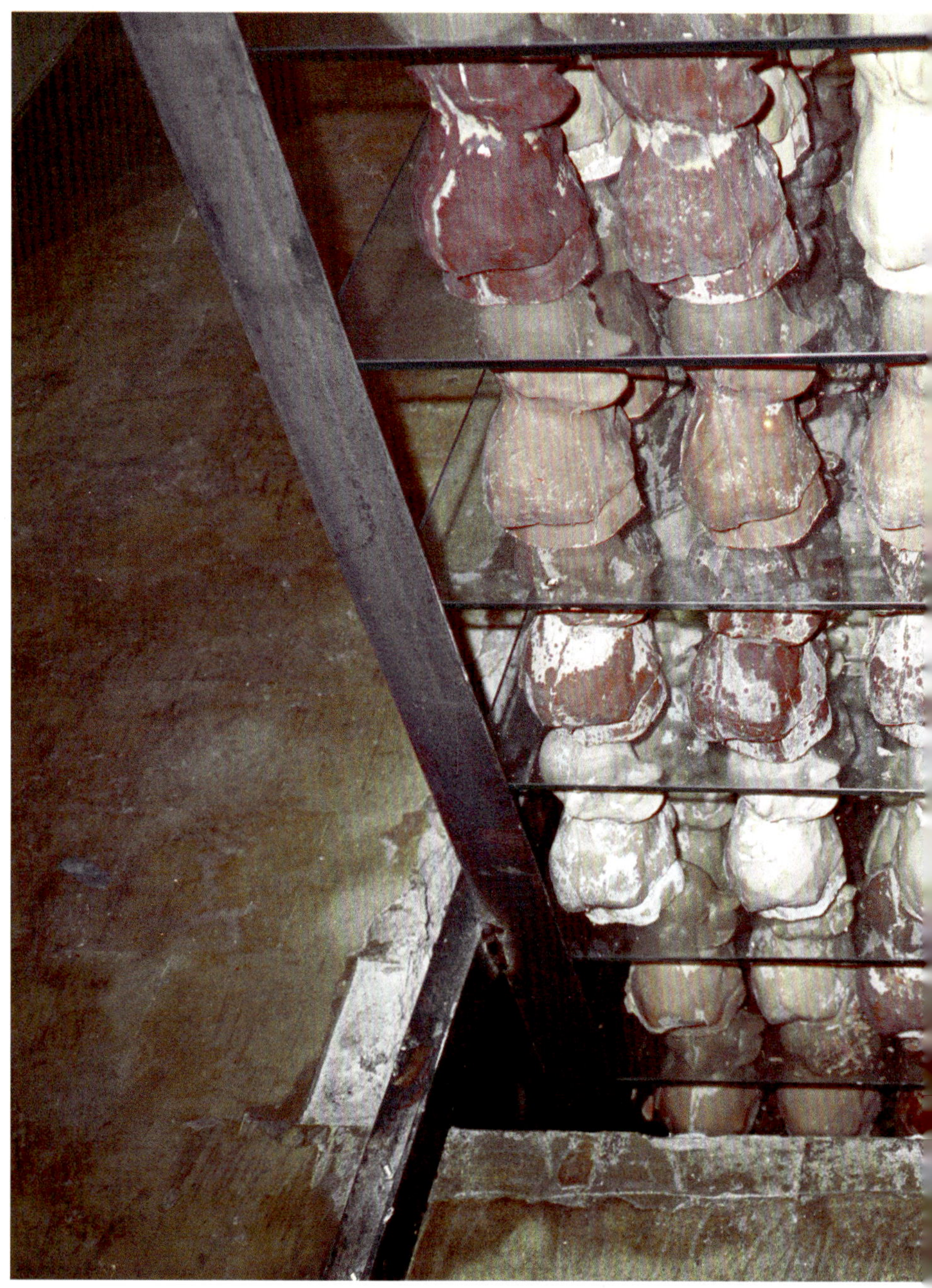

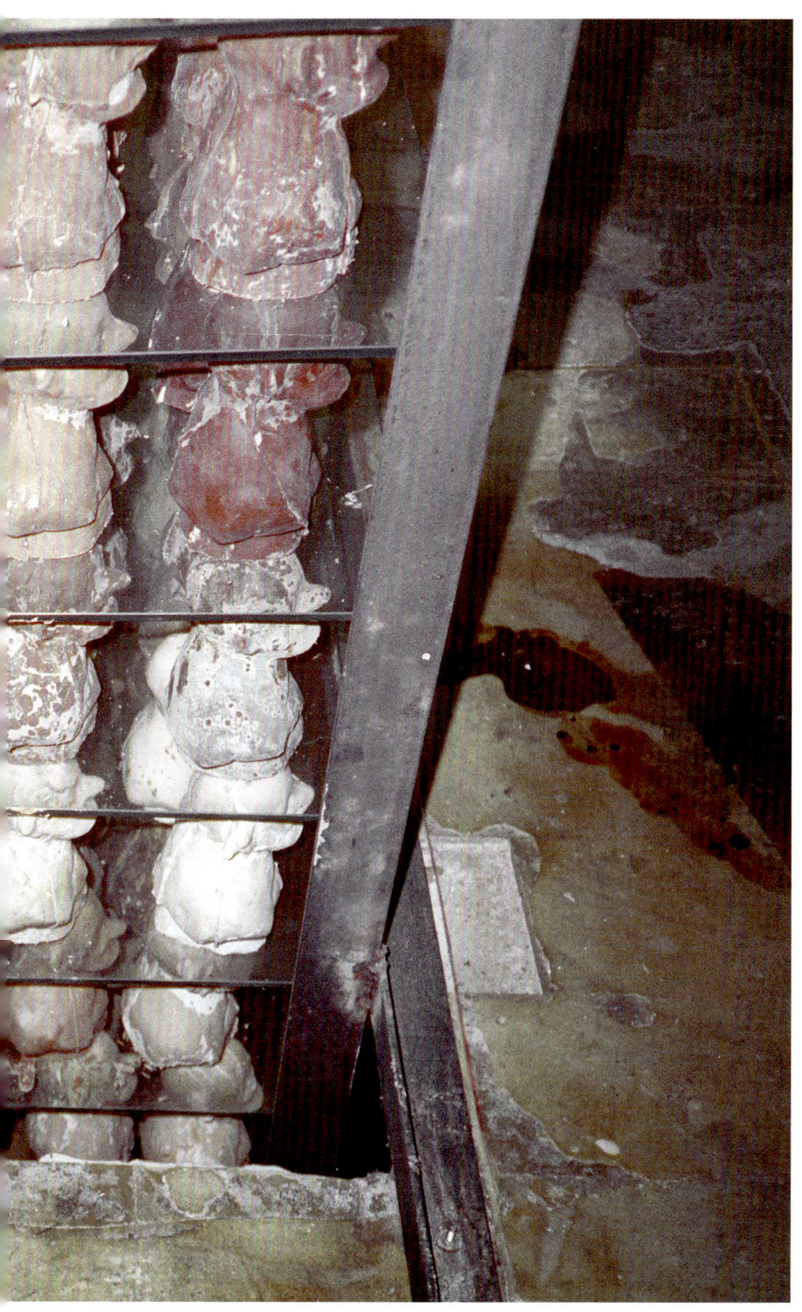

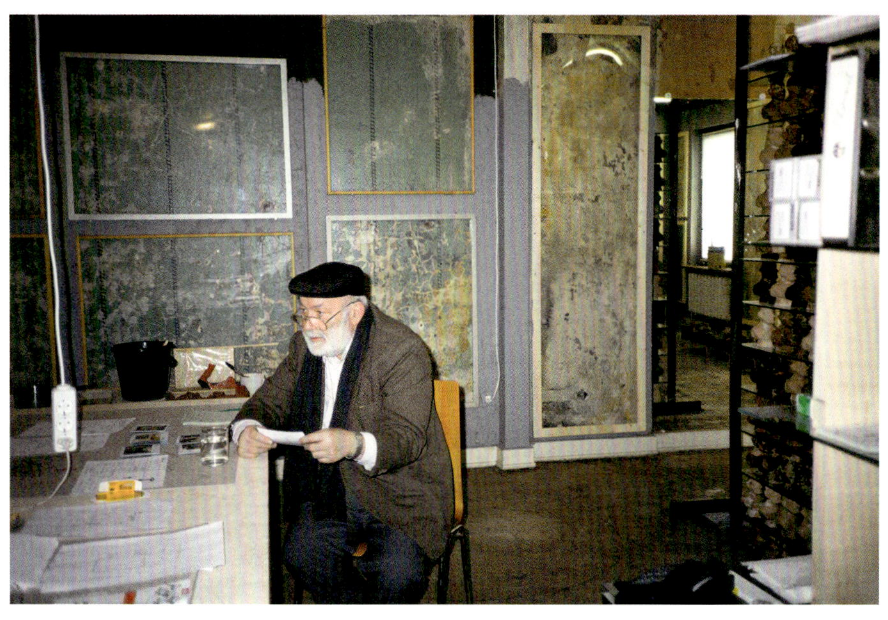

Dieter Roth vor *Fundbilder,* gerahmten Wandausschnitten hinter Plexiglas.
Die ungerahmten Wandflächen sind grau bemalt.
Dieter Roth in front of *Found Pictures,* framed wall cut-outs behind Perspex.
The unframed wall sections are painted grey.

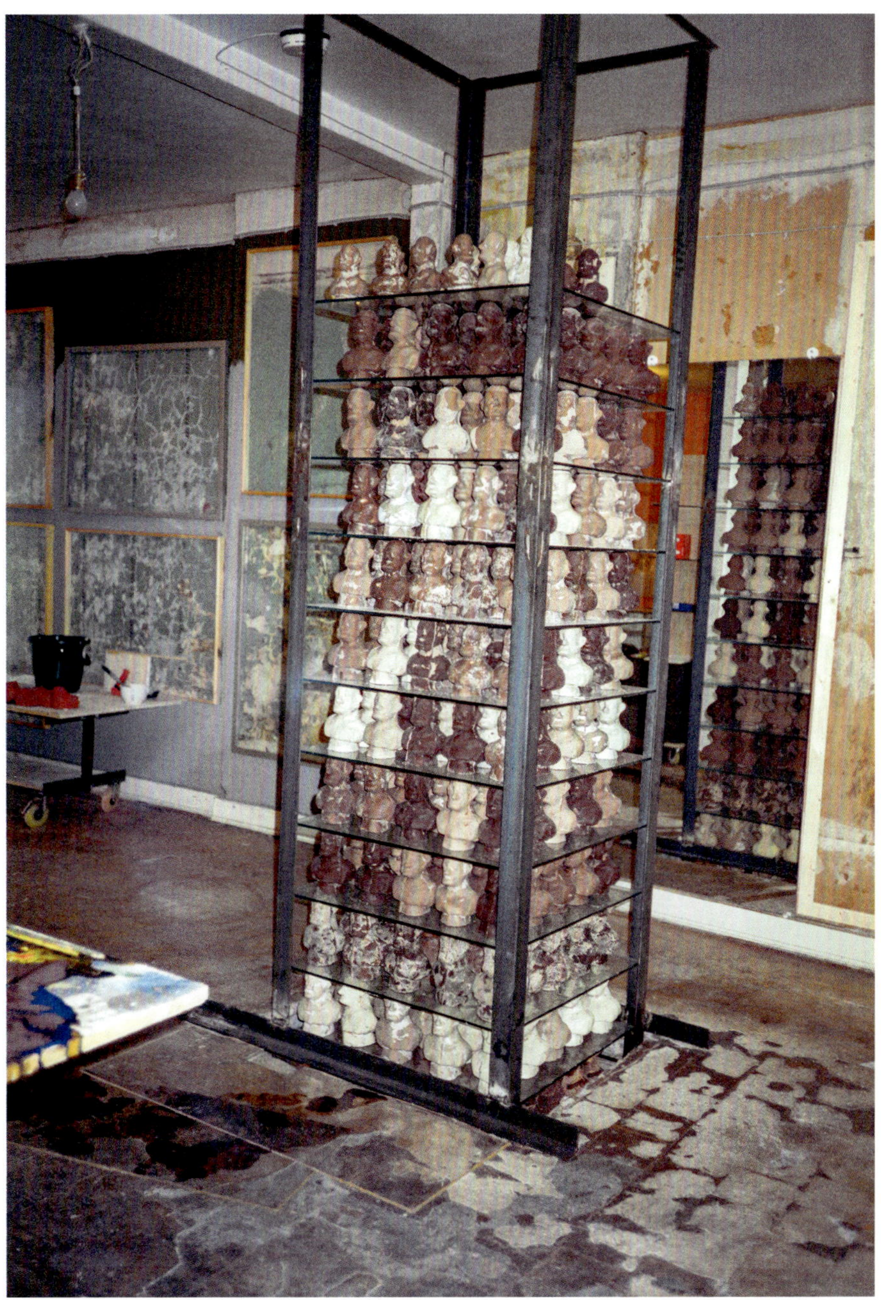

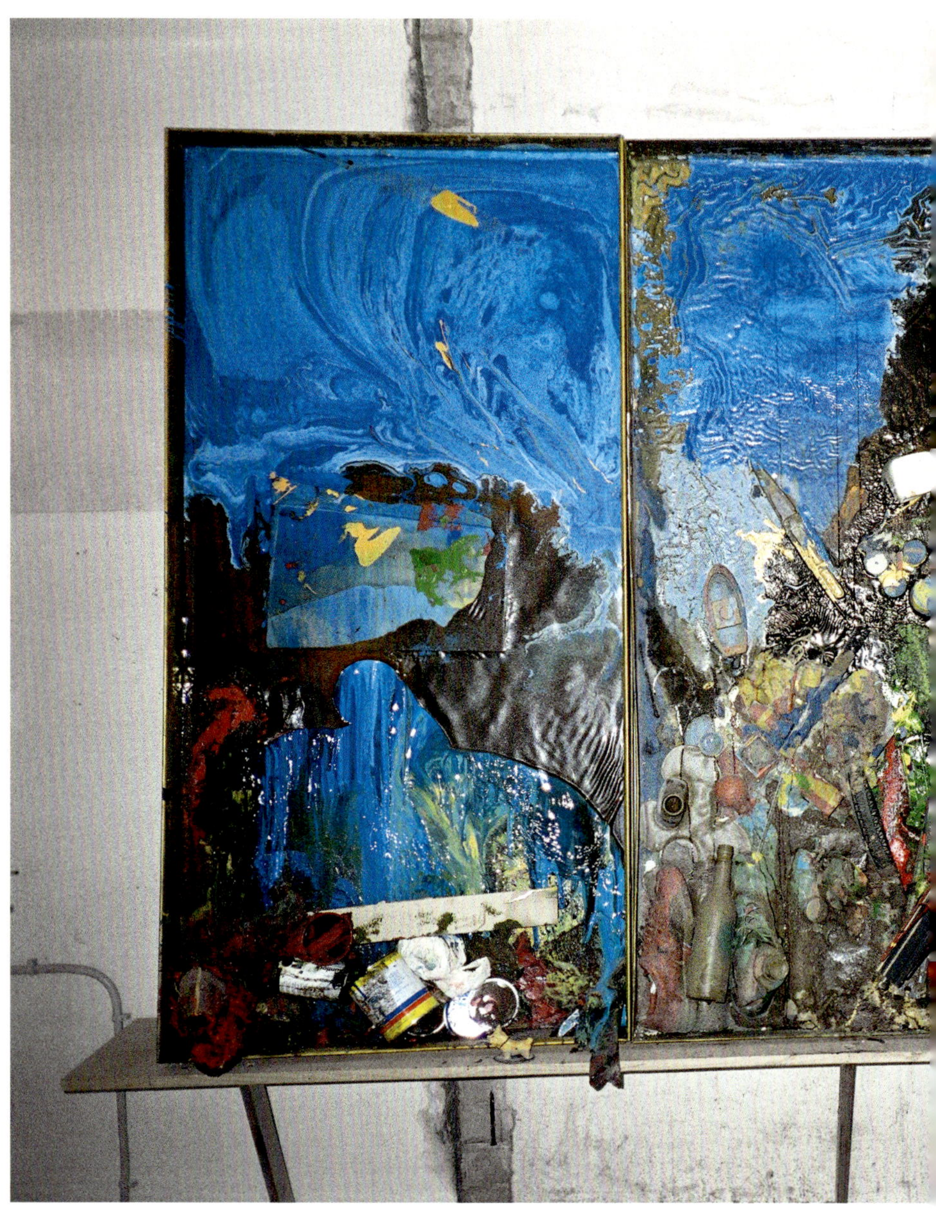

Landschaft mit Turm, Abfälle, Spielzeug, Farbdosen, Malutensilien in 3 Eisenblechwannen.
Landscape with Tower, refuse materials, toy, paint tins, painting utensils in 3 sheet iron tubs.

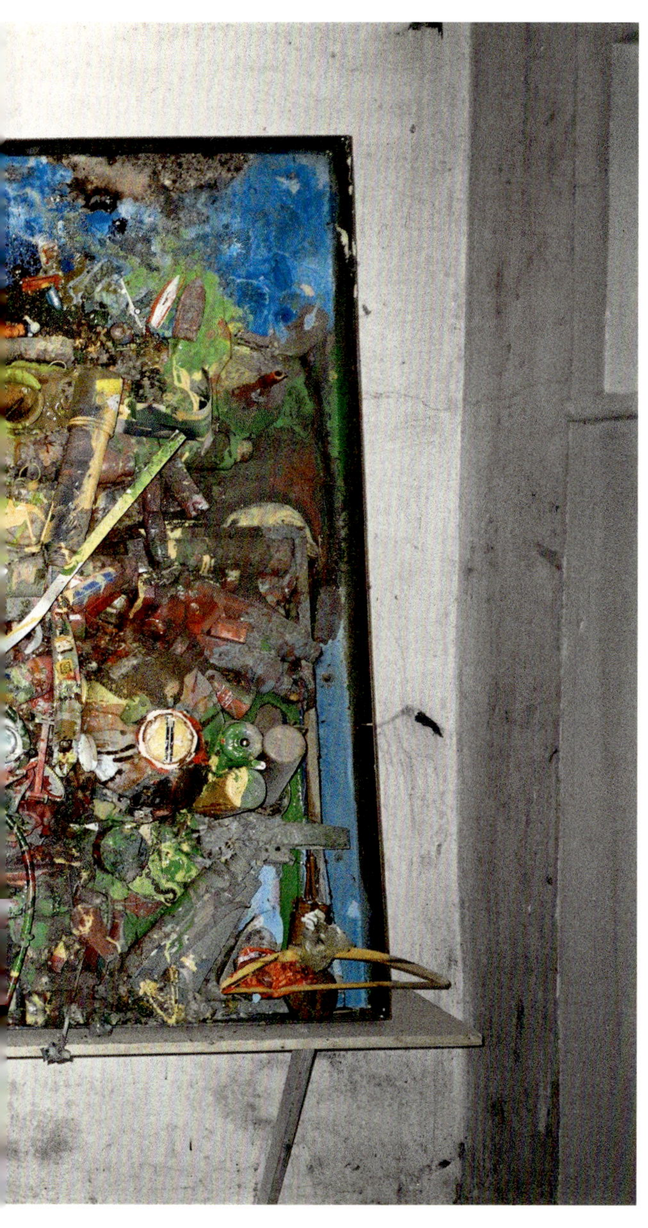

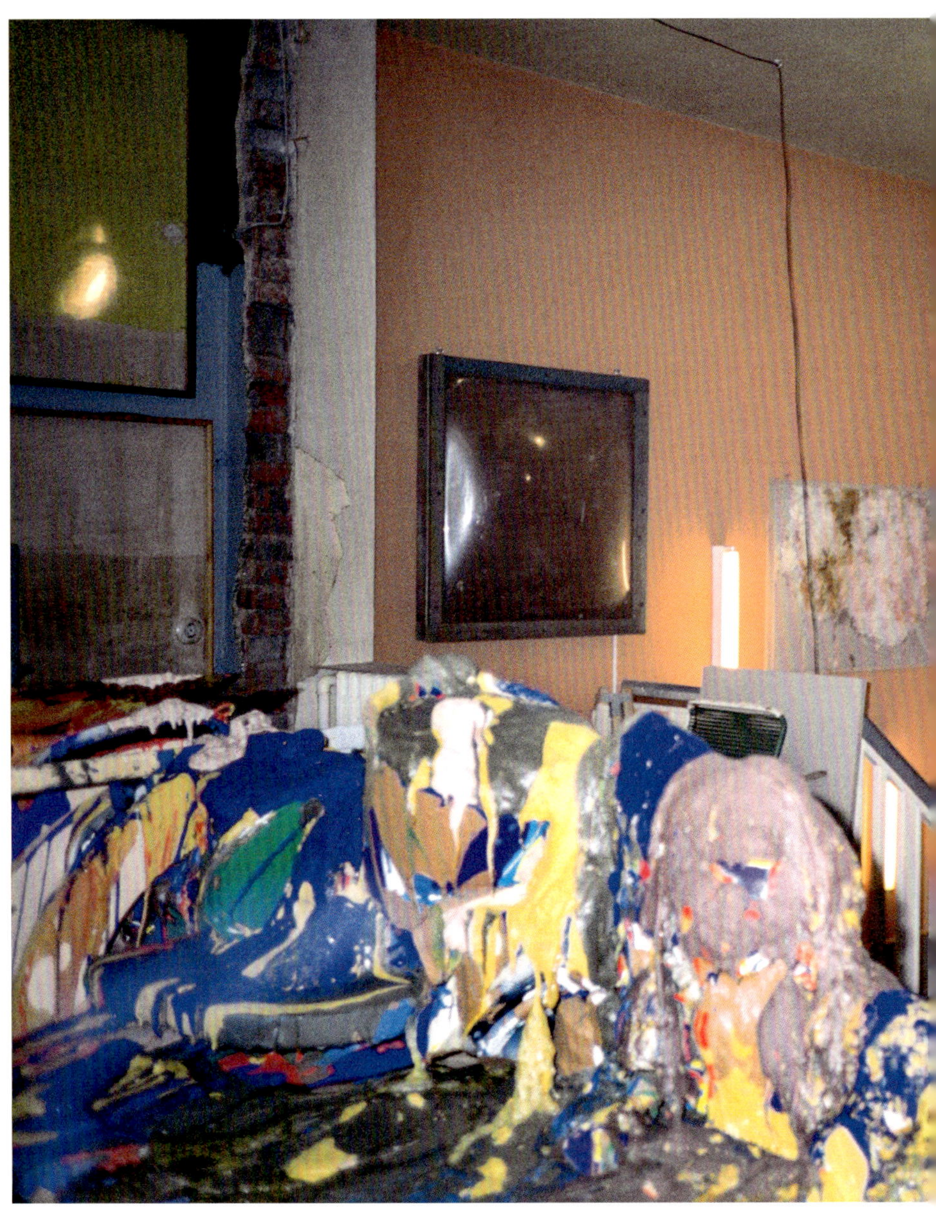

Vorne links: *Haufen,* Acrylfarbe, Brot.
  Front left: *Heap,* acrylic paint, bread.

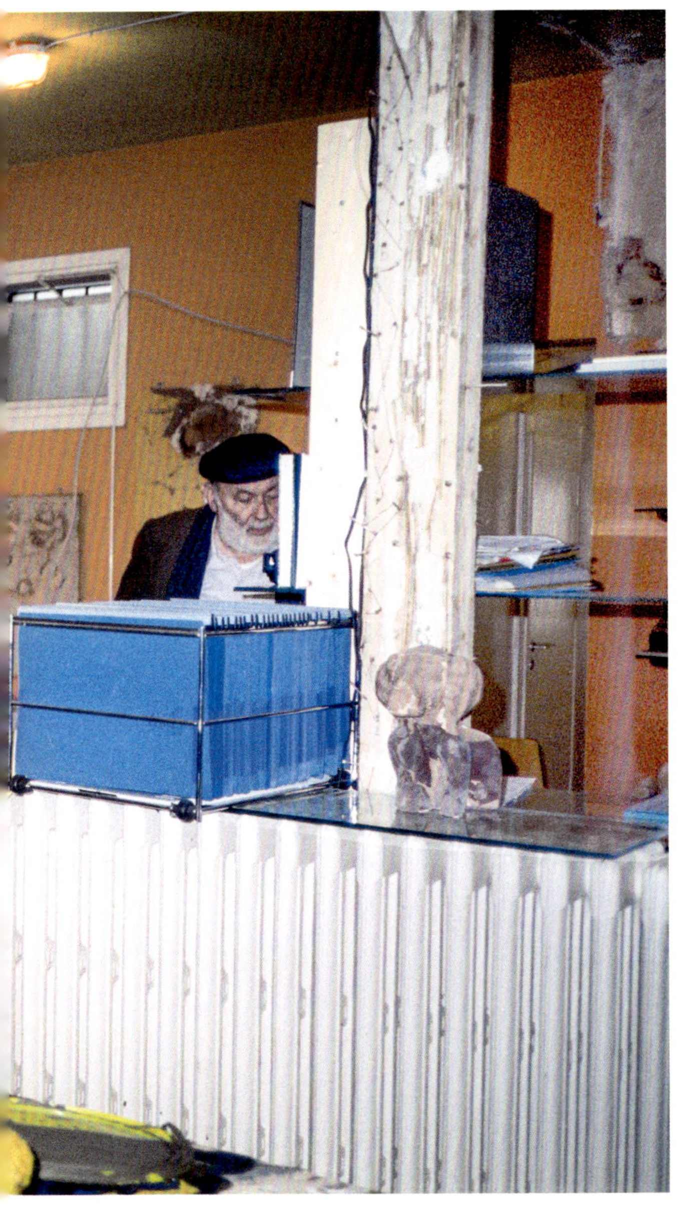

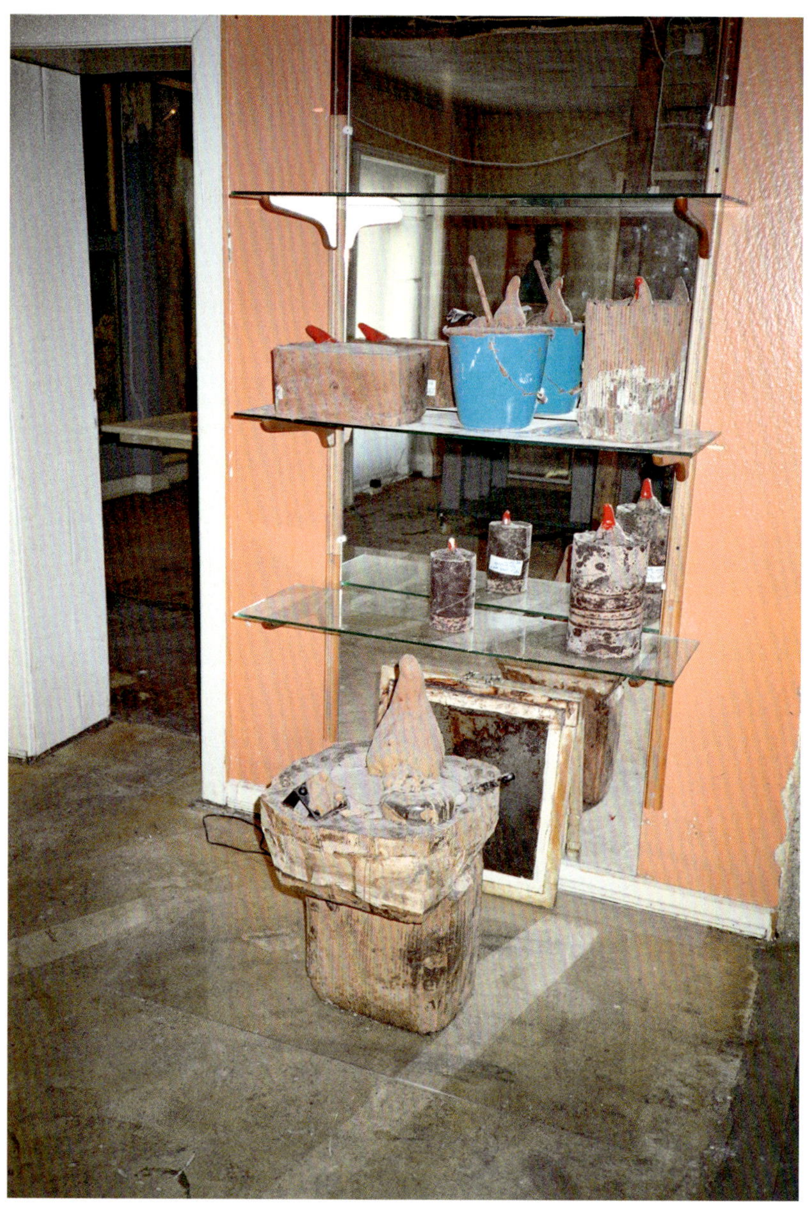

Gartenzwerge, Kunststoffgartenzwerge in Schokolade.
  Garden Gnomes, plastic garden gnomes in chocolate.

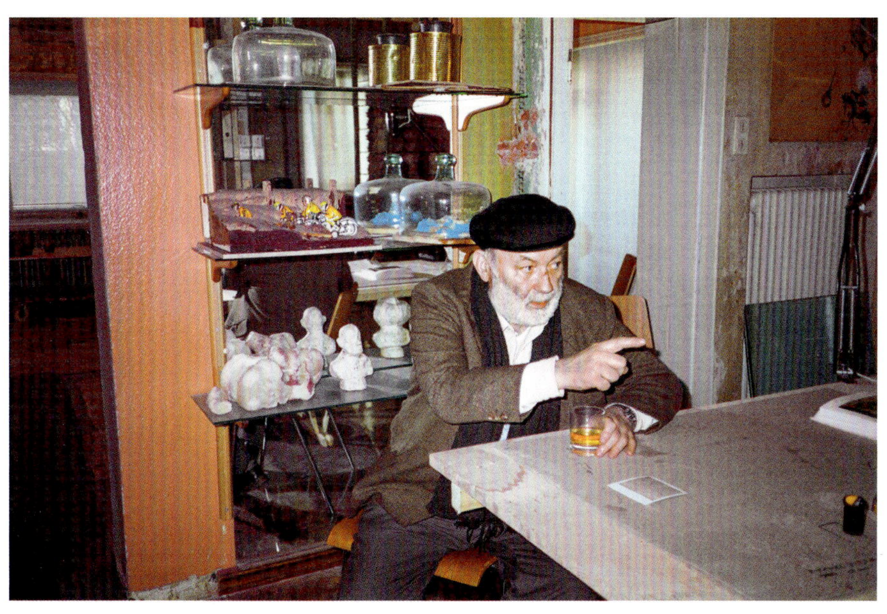

Dieter Roth im ‹Schimmelmuseum›.
Dieter Roth in his Schimmelmuseum.

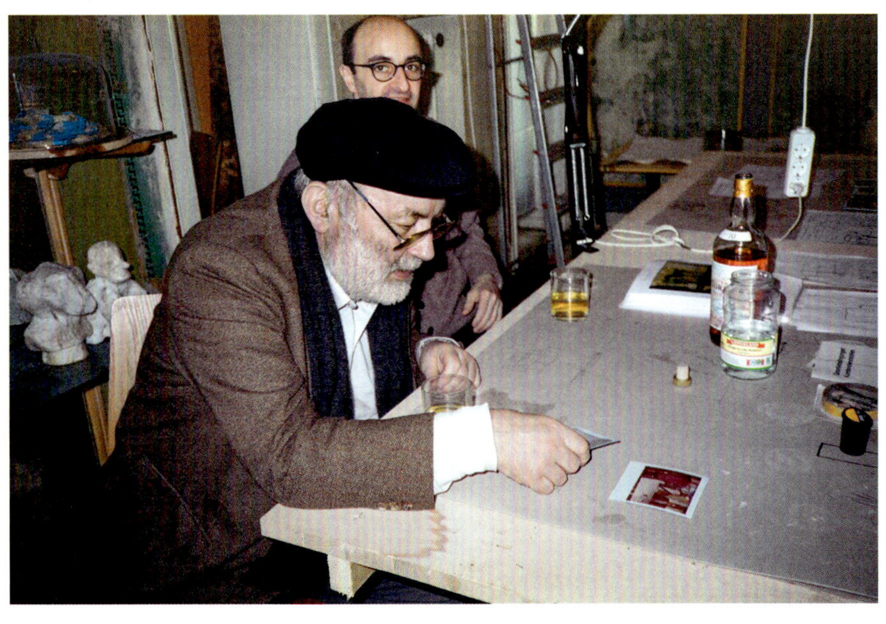

Polaroidporträts der Gäste waren Bestandteil der Installation.
Polaroid portraits of the visitors made up part of the installation.

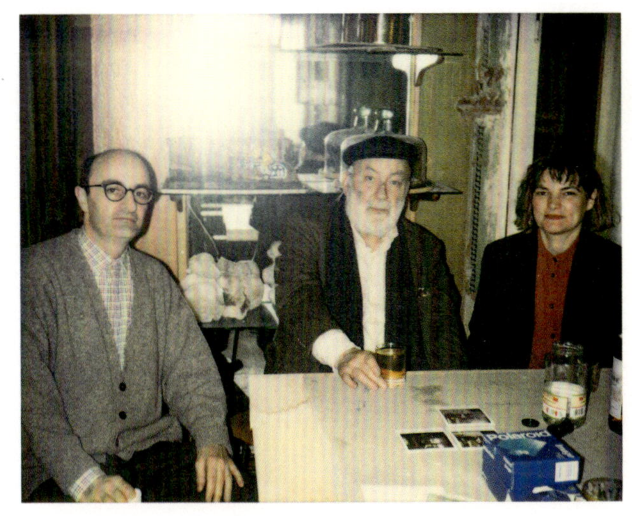

Polaroid, Beat Keusch, Dieter Roth und Erika Streit im ‹Schimmelmuseum›.
Polaroid photo, Beat Keusch, Dieter Roth, and Erika Streit in the Schimmelmuseum.

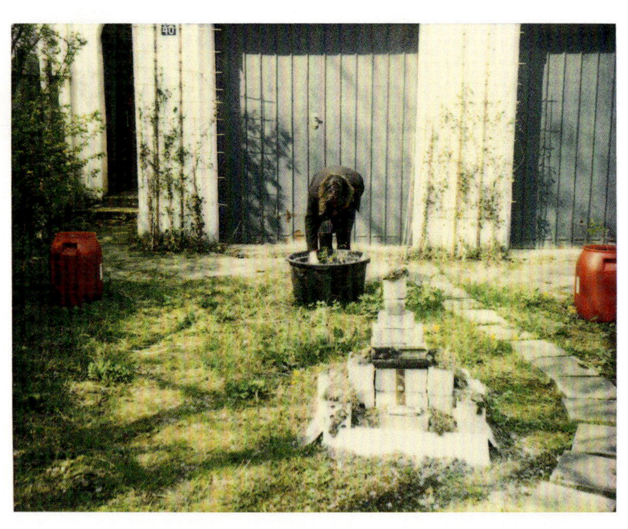

Polaroid, Pflanzen und *(Abfall-)Objekt* im Aussenbereich des ‹Schimmelmuseum›.
Polaroid photo, plants and *(Waste) Object* in the outdoor area of the Schimmelmuseum.

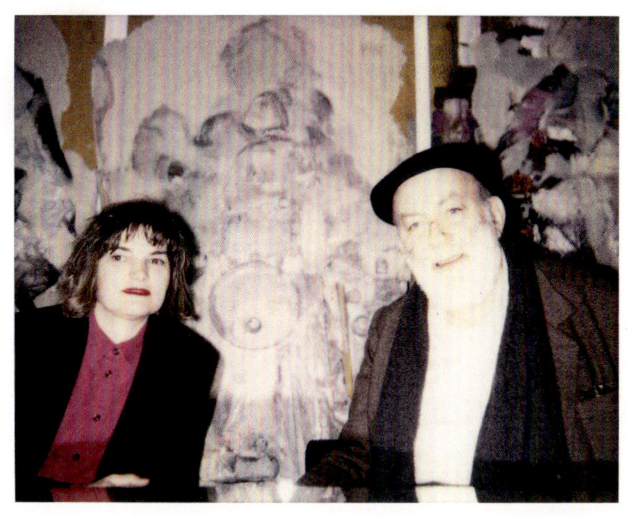

Polaroid, im benachbarten ‹Dieter Roth Museum› vor *Retuschiertes Kleiderbild* und
Gescheckertes Kleiderbild, Kleidungsstücke, Abfall, Leim, Farbe.
 Polariod photo, in the neighbouring Dieter Roth Museum in front of *Retouched Clothes
Picture* and *Chequered Clothes Picture,* garments, refuse, glue, colour.

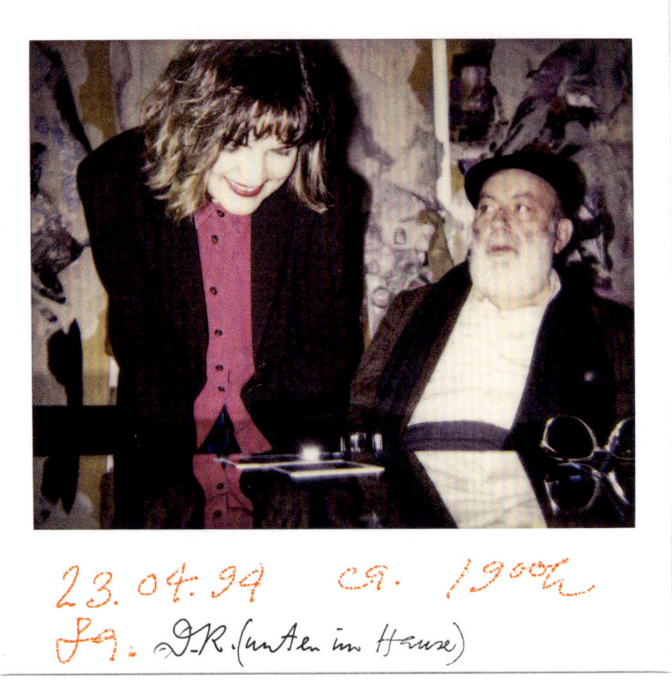

Polaroid, beschriftet von Erika Streit und Dieter Roth.
Polaroid photo, labelled by Erika Streit and Dieter Roth.

Im ‹Roth-Raum› in Basel werden Gussfiguren aus Schokolade
sowie aus Zucker, Lebensmittelfarbe, Acrylfarbe, Tinte
und Tusche auf Glasplatten gestapelt zum *Selbstturm* und zum
Löwenturm. Anhand einer Skizze erklärte uns Dieter Roth
die vier Figurentypen. Kontinuierlich arbeitete er mit seinem
Sohn Björn und weiteren Mitarbeitenden an den beiden
Türmen. Die 1968 begonnene Installation steht seit 1969 in
dem zum Kunstmuseum Basel | Gegenwart gehörenden
‹Roth-Raum›. Die folgenden Fotografien und die Skizze entstanden im November 1995.

In the Roth Room in Basel, figures cast in chocolate,
sugar, food colouring, acrylic paint, ink, and Indian ink are
stacked on glass panes to make up *Self Tower* and *Lion
Tower.* Dieter Roth explained the four figure types to us with
the help of a sketch. Together with his son Björn and other
co-workers he worked continuously on the two towers. The
installation was begun in 1968 and has been standing in
the Roth Room, which makes up part of the Kunstmuseum
Basel | Gegenwart, since 1969. The following photographs
and the sketch were made in 1995.

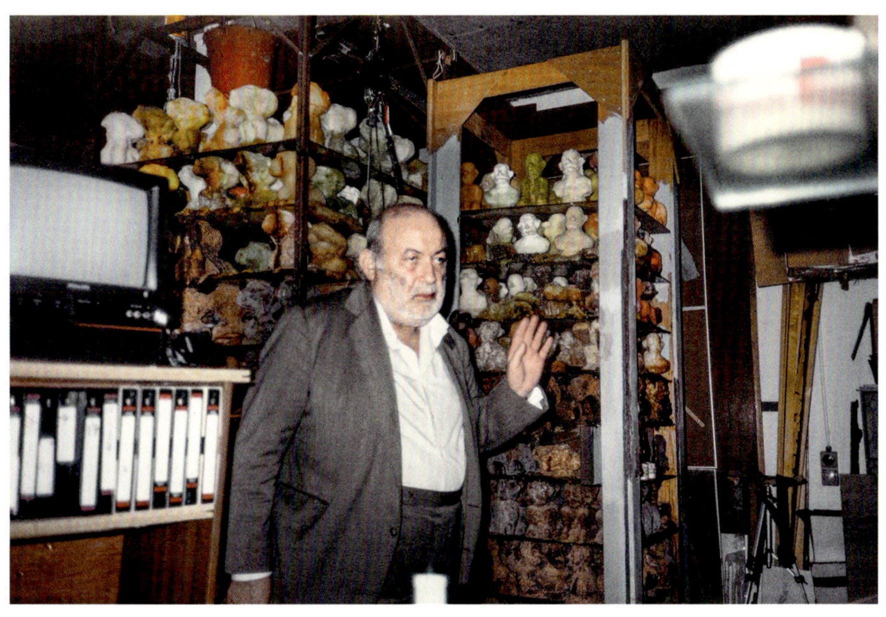

Dieter Roth vor *Löwenturm* und *Selbstturm* im ‹Roth-Raum› am St. Alban-Rheinweg in Basel.
Vorne links: Videokassetten der aufgenommenen Gespräche mit Gästen.
Dieter Roth in front of *Lion Tower* and *Self Tower* in the Roth Room on St. Alban-Rheinweg
in Basel. Front left: video cassettes containing recorded conversations with guests.

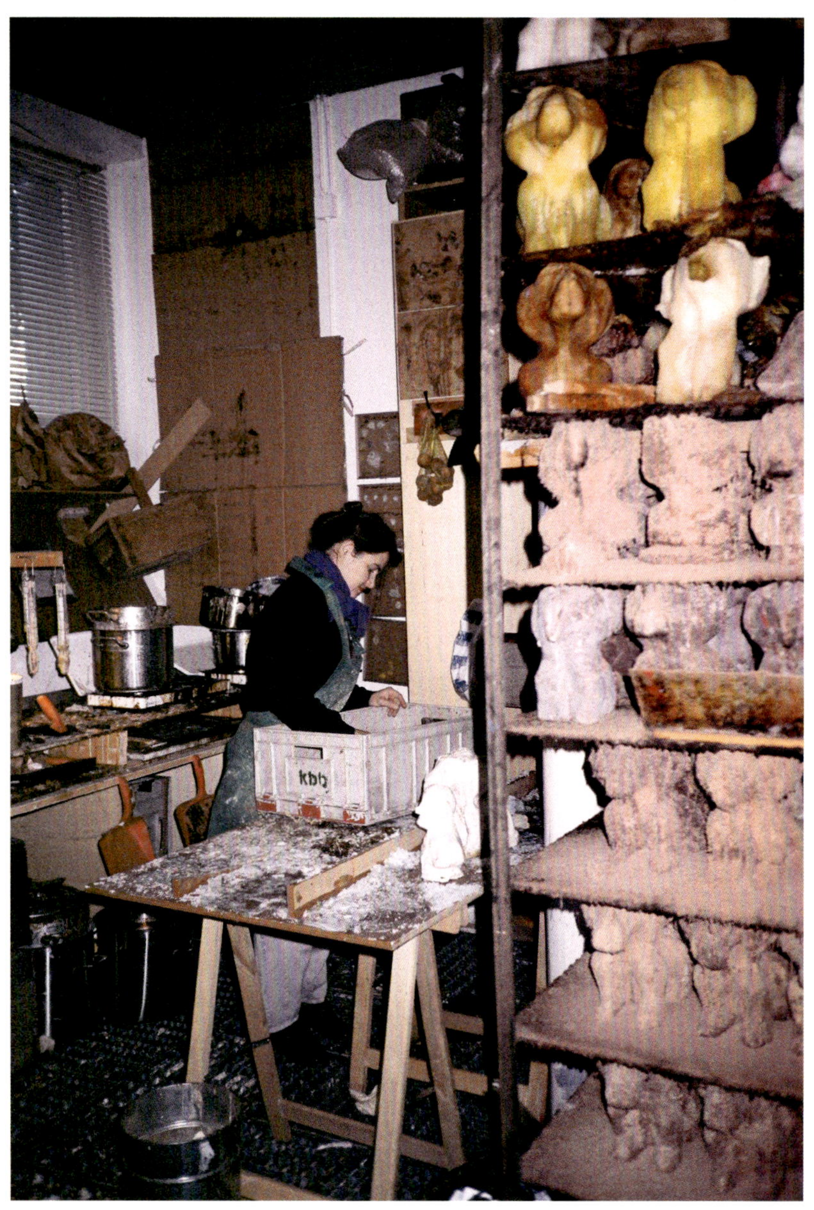

Erika Streit beim Zerhacken der Kuvertüre.
Erika Streit chopping the couverture.

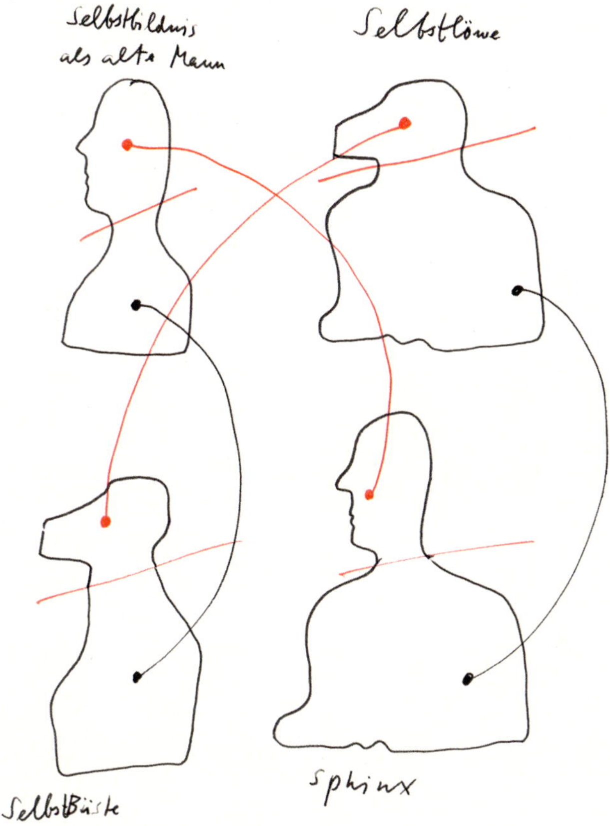

Skizze, *Selbstbildnis als alter Mann, Selbstlöwe, SelbstBüste, Sphinx,* Filzstift.
Sketch, *Self-portrait as an Old Man, Self Lion, Self Bust, Sphinx,* felt-tip pen.

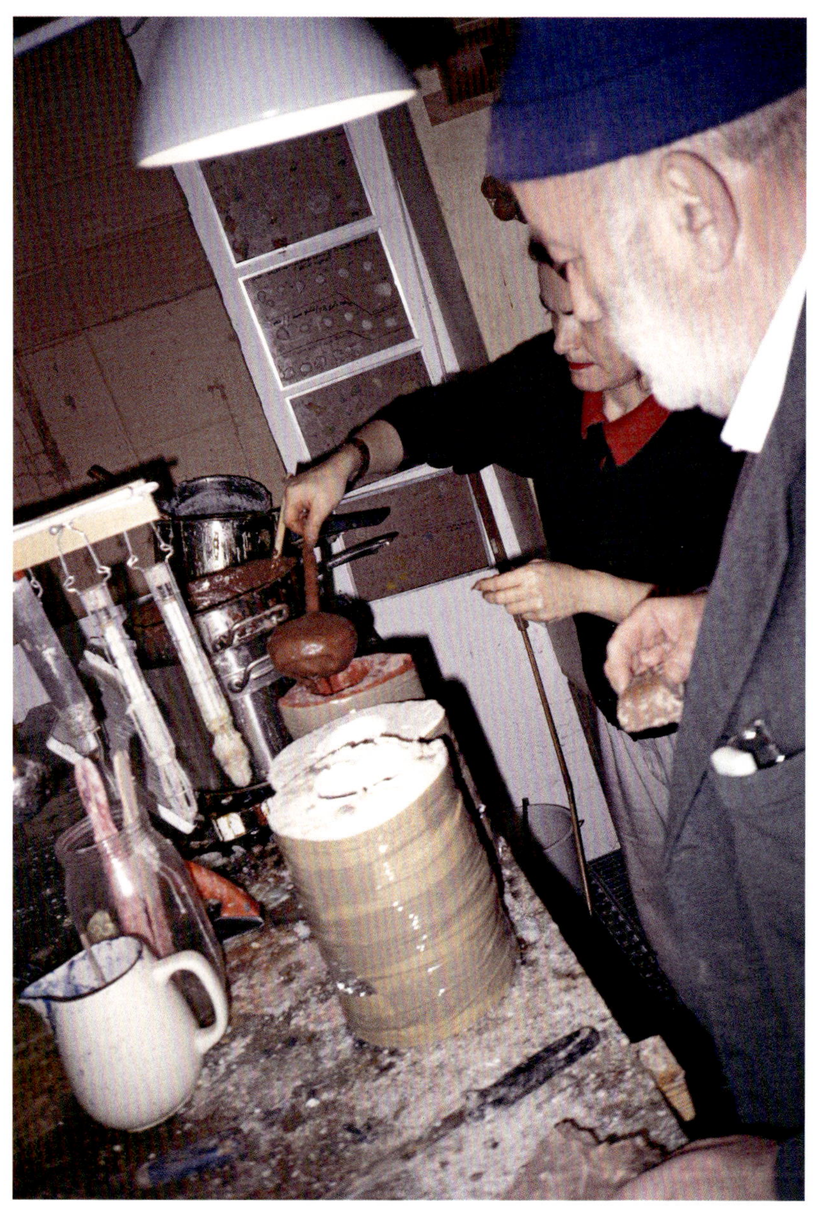

Erika Streit und Dieter Roth beim Figurengiessen.
Erika Streit and Dieter Roth casting figures.

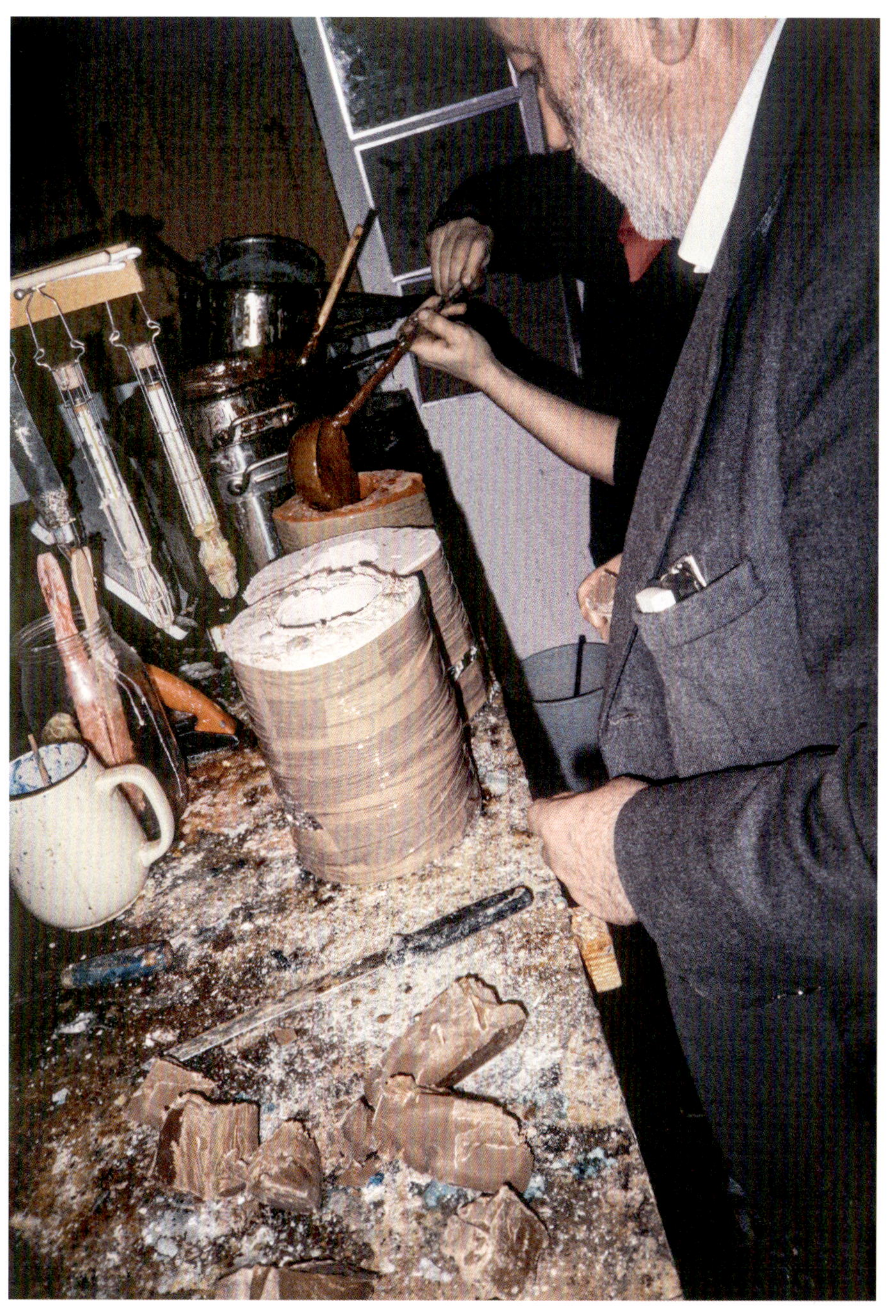

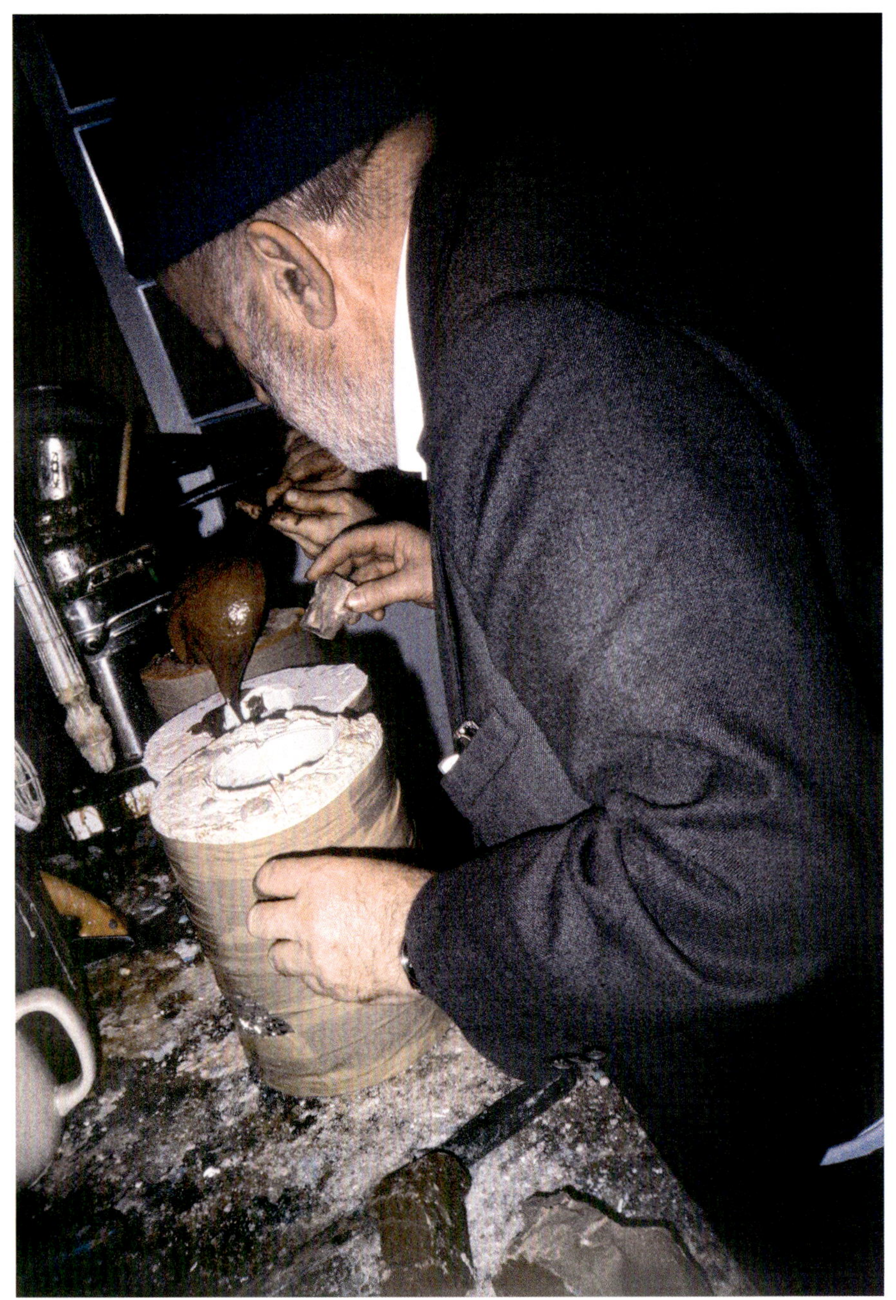

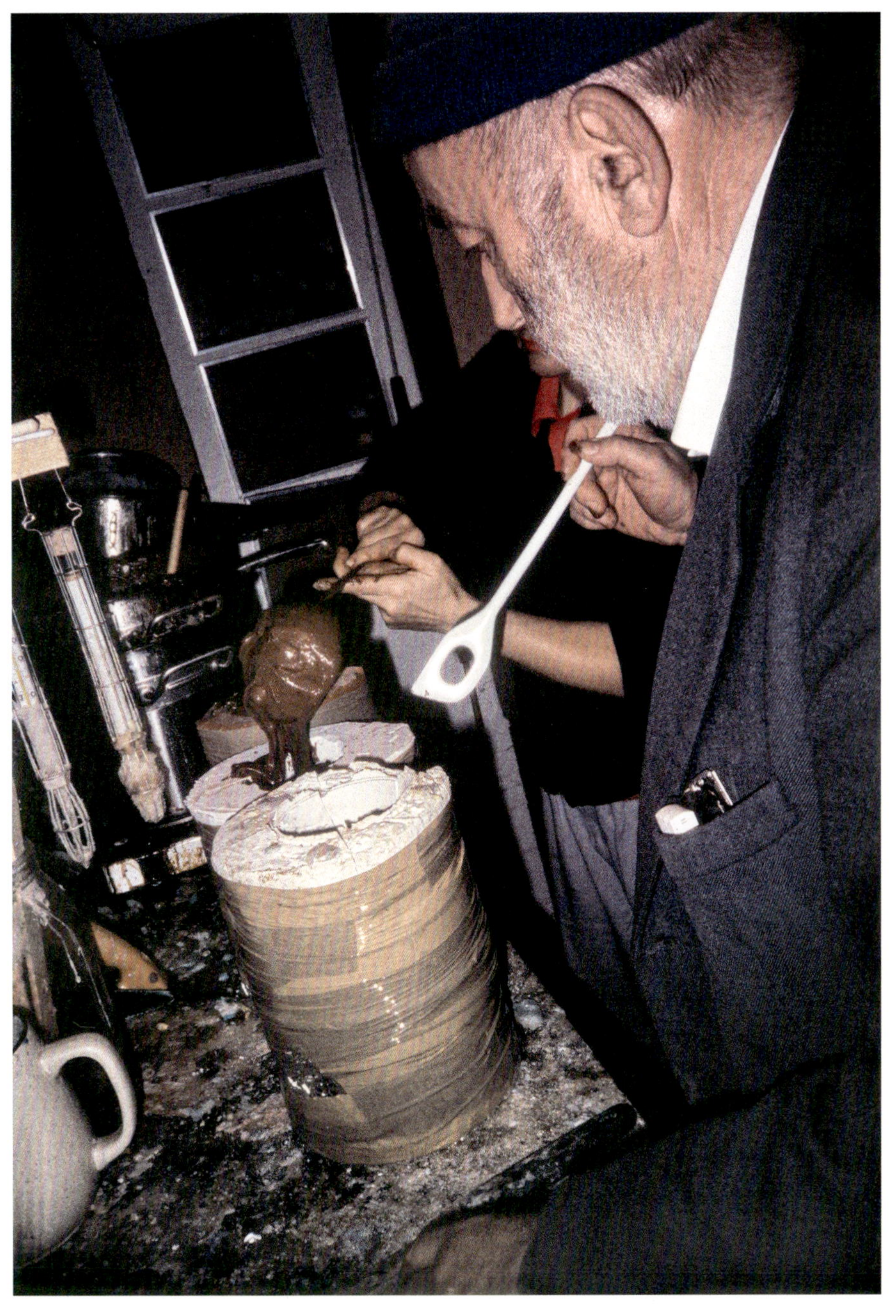

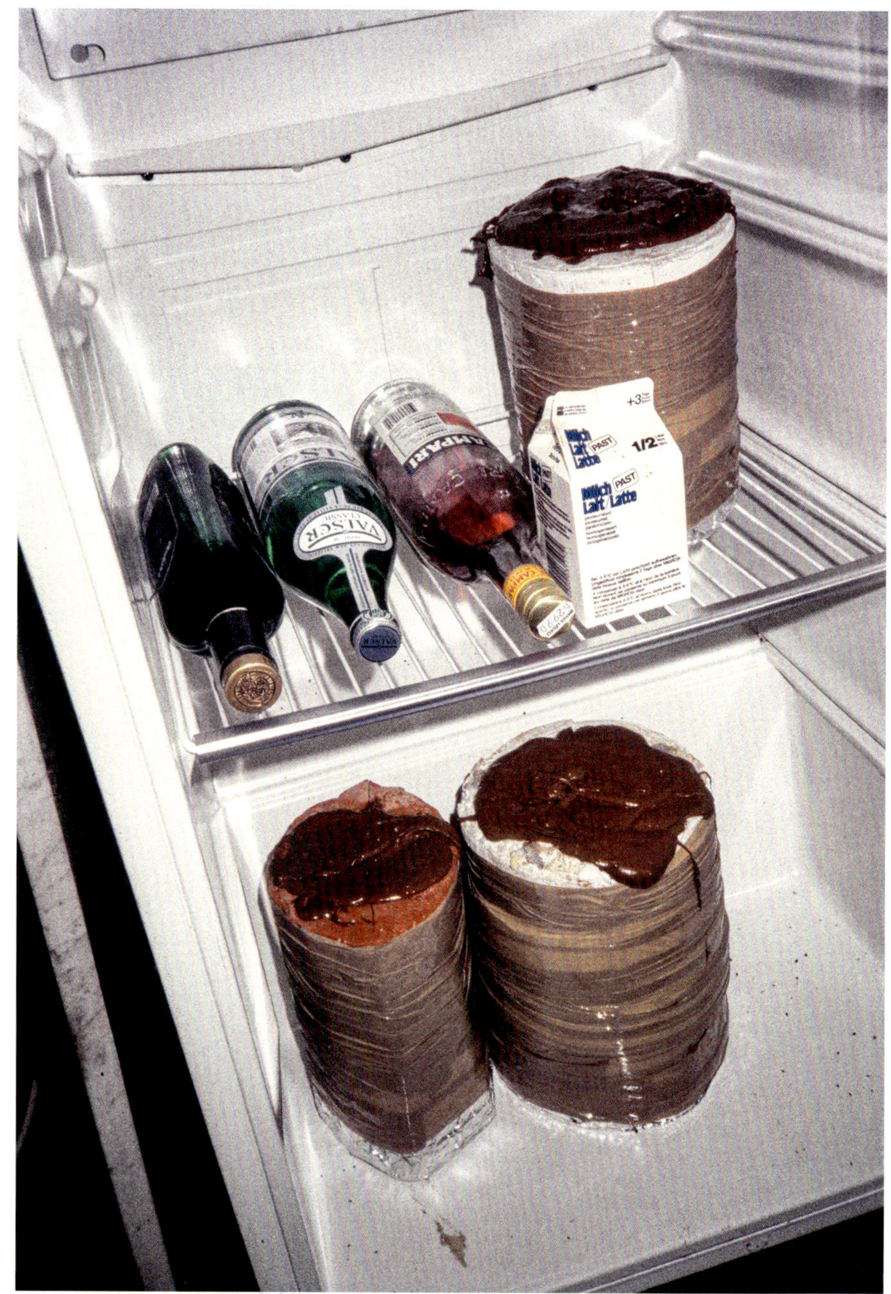

VALSER
CLASSIC
CAMPARI
Milch Lait Latte PAST +3
1/2

Bevor wir auf Einladung Dieter Roths nach Island reisten,
schickte er uns ein Fax mit einem symmetrischen Text, in
dem er uns bittet, eine Kamera aus seinem Atelier in Basel
mitzubringen. Der Text entstand als einer von sieben Bei-
trägen für eine Radiosendung von Fredie Beckmans, einem
Bekannten Dieter Roths in Amsterdam. Die Serie bestand
in Erweiterungen von Geschichten mit der einen Bedingung,
dass der letzte Satz dasselbe aussagt wie der erste.

Before we travelled to Iceland following Dieter Roth's
invitation, he sent us a fax with a symmetrical text in which
he asked us to bring with us a camera from his studio in
Basel. The text was created as one of seven contributions for
a radio broadcast by Fredie Beckmans, a friend of his in
Amsterdam. The series consisted of add-on stories that were
subject to one condition only, namely that the last sentence
carried the same message as the first.

Story for Fredie Beckmans
Beat, best bring the camera along with you when you come. Michael will bring it to you;
it's still lying (or standing) in my studio in Sankt Johanns Vorstadt. We, i.e. Björn and I,
do have a camera here, but the flash doesn't work, and it would, or could, take a long while
to have it fixed. It's the dark season here. But it would take quite some time to have the
camera repaired, that is, I would have to wait a long time to get the camera back. The flash no
longer works on the camera we, meaning Björn and I, have here. A camera, my camera is
still standing (or lying) in Sankt Johanns Vorstadt, in my studio. Michael will bring it to you.
If you were to bring it along with you on your visit to us, that would be the best thing, Beat.
Bala, 07.02.'97   1 kind greeting!   Dieter Roth

Geschichte z. Hd.   ~~[gestrichen]~~
                Fredie Beckmans

Beat, am Besten, Ihr bringt die Kamera
mit wenn Ihr kommt. Der Michael wird sie
Dir bringen; sie liegt noch (oder steht) in
meine Wohnung an der Sankt Johanns
Vorstadt. Wir, Björn & ich, haben wohl
eine Kamera hier, aber der Flash wirkt
nicht; bis der repariert ist, kann bzw. wird
viel Zeit vergehen. In dieser dunklen
Jahreszeit brauche ich einen Flash, sonst
ist es auf den Bildern dann dunkel.
Das ist diese dunkle Jahreszeit. Jedoch
es verginge zuviel Zeit, brächte ich die
Kamera zur Reparatur bzw. müsste auf
die Kamera lange warten. Der Flash
wirkt nicht an jener Kamera die wir,
Björn und ich, hier haben. Eine, meine,
Kamera steht (oder liegt) noch an der
~~[gestrichen]~~ Sankt Johanns Vorstadt in meiner
Wohnung; der Michael wird sie Dir
bringen. Wenn Ihr sie mitbringt, auf
Eurer Reise zu uns, dann ist das
das Beste, Beat.

Basel, 07.02.97

1 schönen Gruss!   Dieter

Mit einer Skizze plante Dieter Roth (D) unsere (B&E) gemein-
same Reise auf Island vom 13. bis 17. Februar 1997. In dieser
Zeit begegneten wir seinem engsten Kreis: Dem Sohn Björn
(Bö), dessen intensive Arbeit mit seinem Vater an den Werken
über die Lebenszeit von Dieter Roth hinausführt. Dem Künst-
ler Jan Voss (Jan), der mit den Künstlerinnen Henriëtte van
Egten und Rúna Thorkelsdóttir den Ausstellungsraum und
Kunstbuchladen ‹Boekie Woekie› in Amsterdam betreibt,
und Gunnar Helgason (Gu), der beim Bauen, Reparieren und
Verändern von Dieter Roths Räumen dessen Vertrauter war.

Dieter Roth (D) drafted our (B&E) joint journey across
Iceland from 13 to 17 February 1997 with the help of a sketch.
On this occasion, we also got to know his inner circle:
his son Björn (Bö) whose close collaboration with his father
extended beyond the life of Dieter Roth; the artist Jan
Voss (Jan), who runs the exhibition space and art bookstore
Boekie Woekie in Amsterdam together with the artists
Henriëtte van Egten and Rúna Thorkelsdóttir, and Gunnar
Helgason (Gu), Dieter Roth's close associate in building,
repairing, and transforming his living spaces.

Skizze, Dieter Roths Vorschlag (isländisch ‹tillaga›) für die Reise.
  Sketch, Dieter Roth's proposal (Icelandic *tillaga*) for the journey.

(B&E), D, (Bö)	Reykjavík	→	Skaftafell	THU	13. Februar	Hotel ①
B&E, D, Bö	Skaftafell	→	Egilstaðir	FRY	14.	"
Jan	Akureyri	→	Egilstaðir	FRY	14.	"
Bö	Egilstaðir	→	Reykjavík	FRY	14.	"
B&E, D, Jan	Egilstaðir	→	Seyðisfjörður	FRY	14.	Bryggjuhús
(B&E), (D), Jan	Seyðisfjörður	→	Akureyri	SAT	15.	Hotel ②
Gu	Reykjavík	→	Akureyri	SUN	16.	"
B&E, D, Jan, Gu	Akureyri	→	Hjalteyri	SUN	16.	"
(B&E), (D), (Gu)	Hjalteyri	→	Akureyri	SUN	16.	Hotel ②
B&E, D, Gu	Akureyri	→	Reykjavík	MON	17.	"

(tillaga)

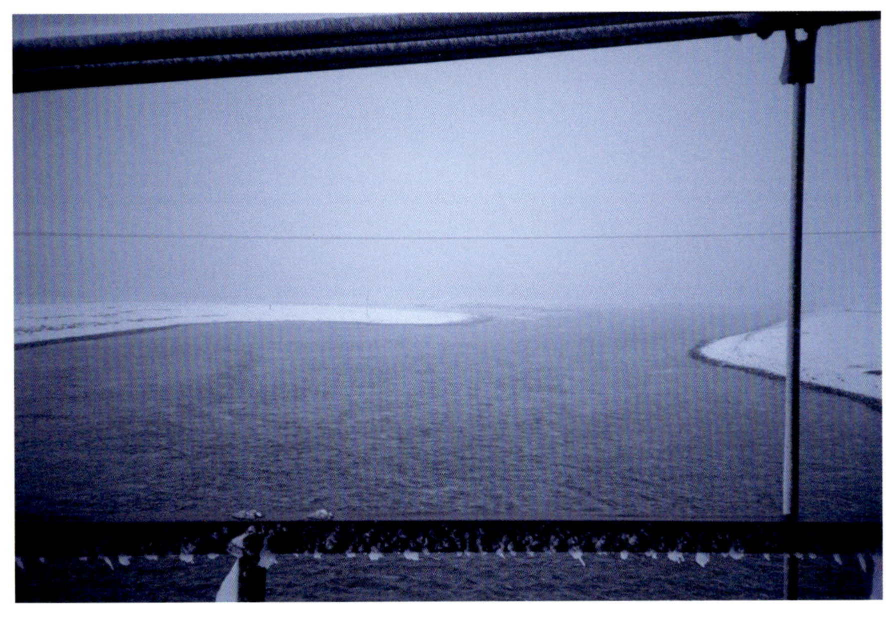

Unter dem Gletscher Breiðamerkurjökull, Südostküste am offenen
Nordatlantik, 13. Februar 1997.
Under the glacier Breiðamerkurjökull, south-east coast looking out towards
the North Atlantic Ocean, 13 February 1997.

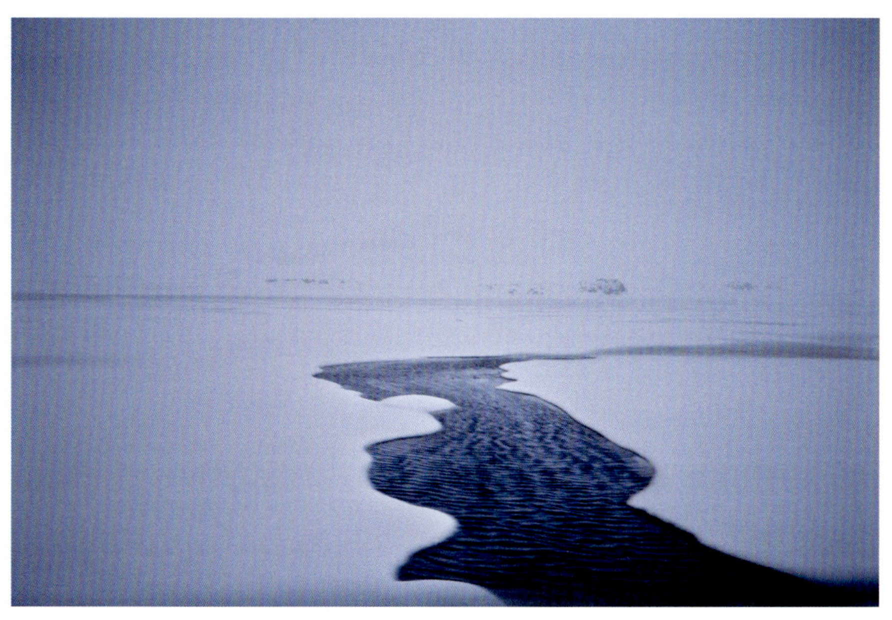

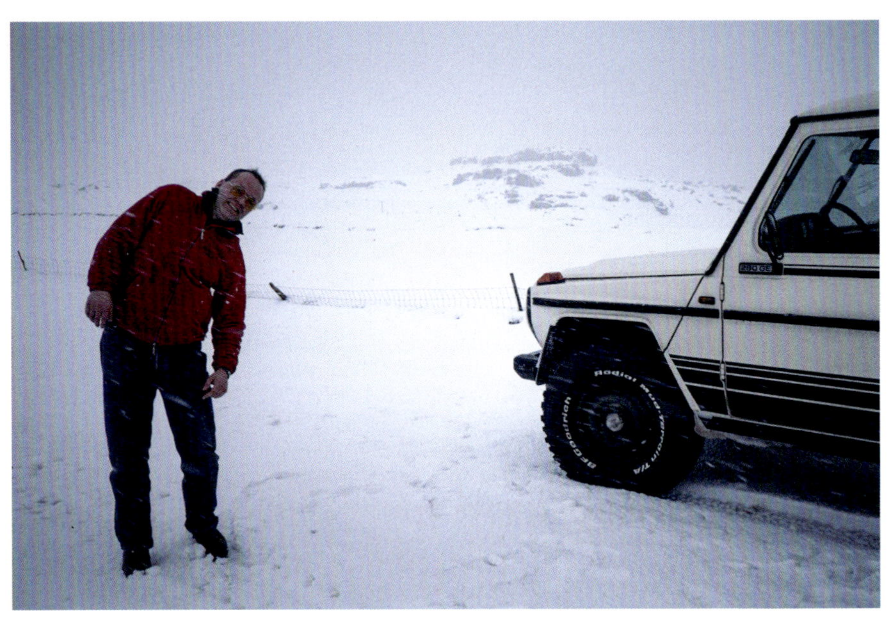

Björn Roth in Suðursveit an der Südostküste.
Björn Roth in Suðursveit on the south-east coast.

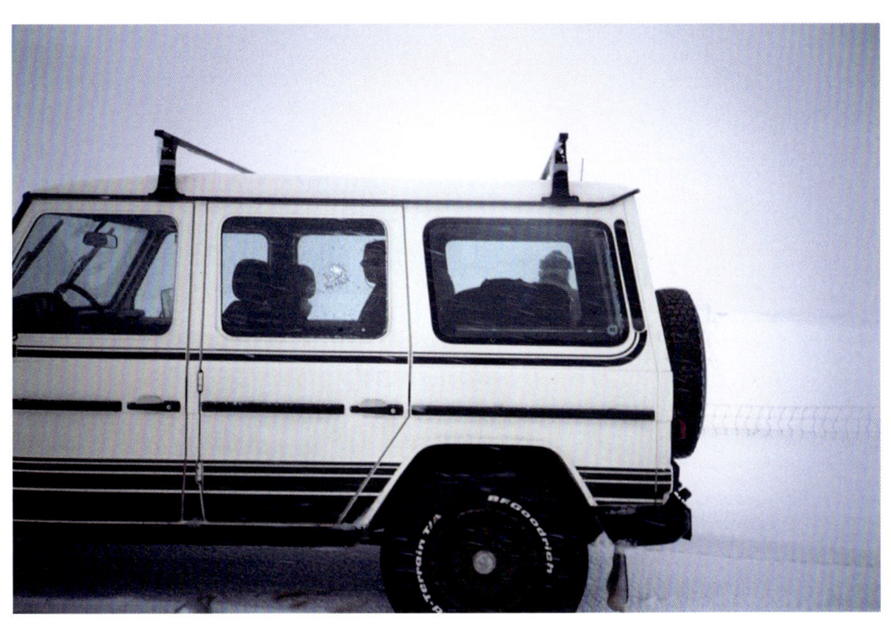

Erika Streit und Dieter Roth suchen den Weg.
Erika Streit and Dieter Roth looking for the way.

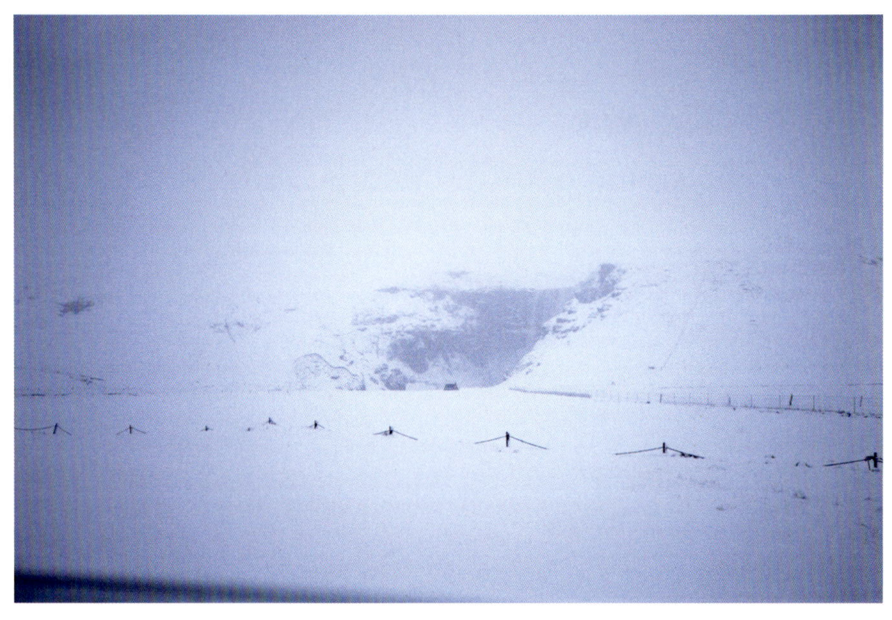

Am Wasserfall Skógarfoss unter dem Gletscher Eyjafjallajökull an der Südküste.
At the waterfall Skógarfoss under the glacier Eyjafjallajökull on the south coast.

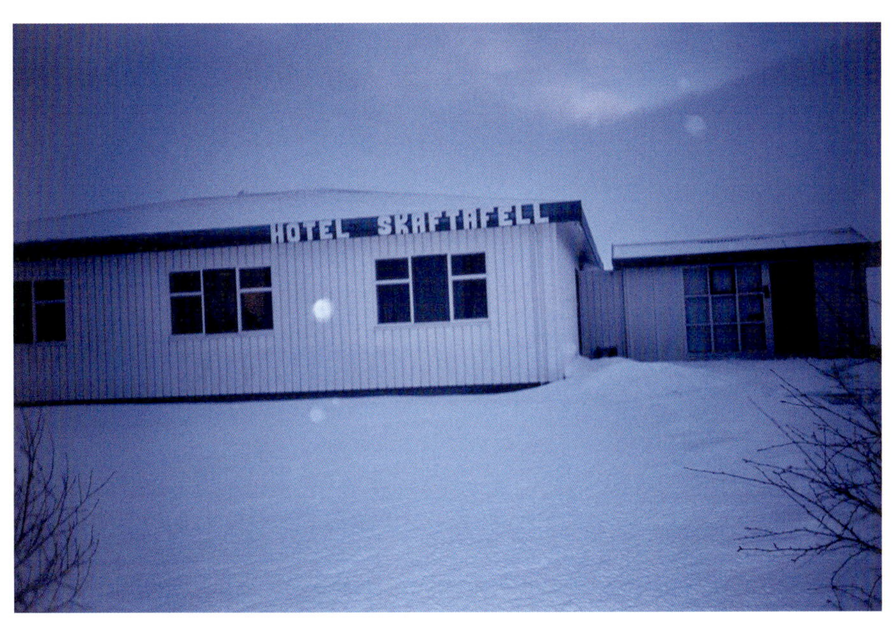

Unter dem Gletscher Vatnajökull, Südostküste.
Under the glacier Vatnajökull, south-east coast.

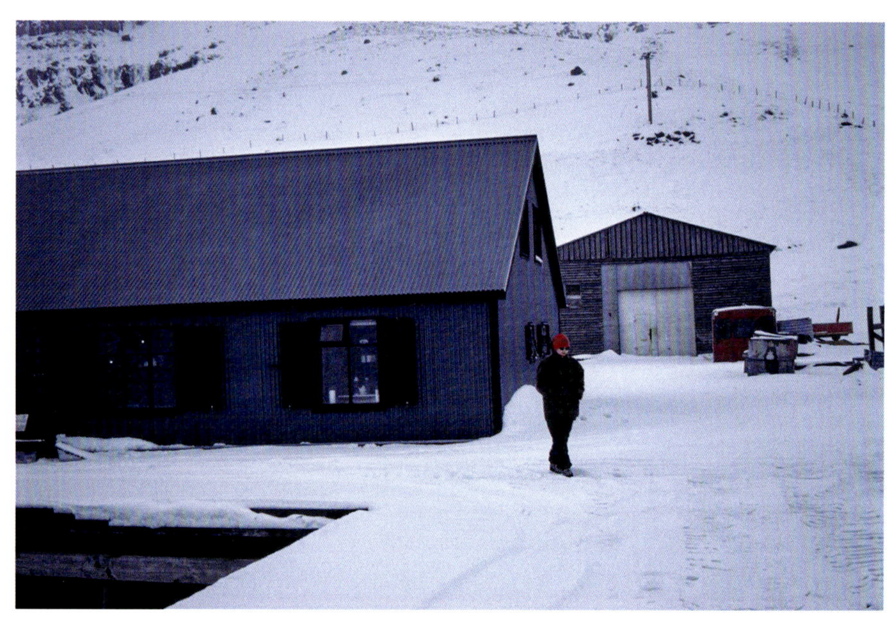

Erika Streit vor Dieter und Björn Roths Bryggjuhús in Seyðisfjörður,
14. Februar 1997.
     Erika Streit in front of Dieter and Björn Roth's Bryggjuhús in Seyðisfjörður,
     14 February 1997.

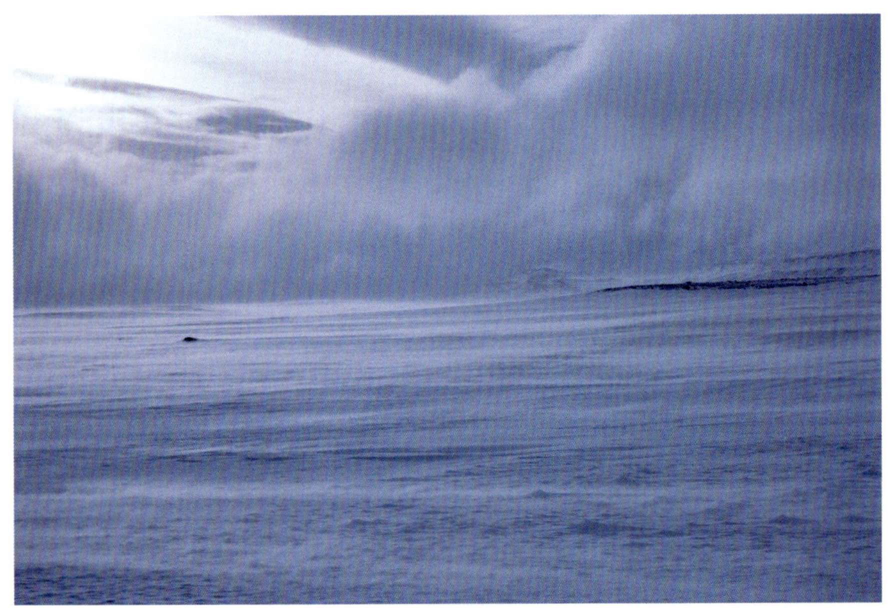

Die Passstrasse Fjarðarheiði nach Seyðisfjörður an den Ostfjorden,
15. Februar 1997.
    The mountain path from Fjarðarheiði to Seyðisfjörður on the eastern fjords,
    15 February 1997.

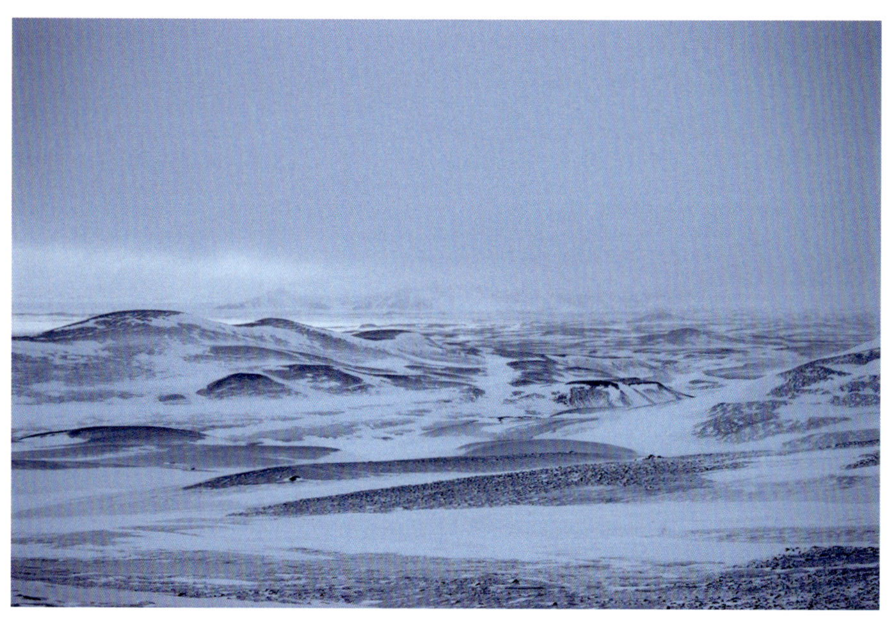

Möðrudalur, nordöstliche Highlands.
Möðrudalur, north-eastern highlands.

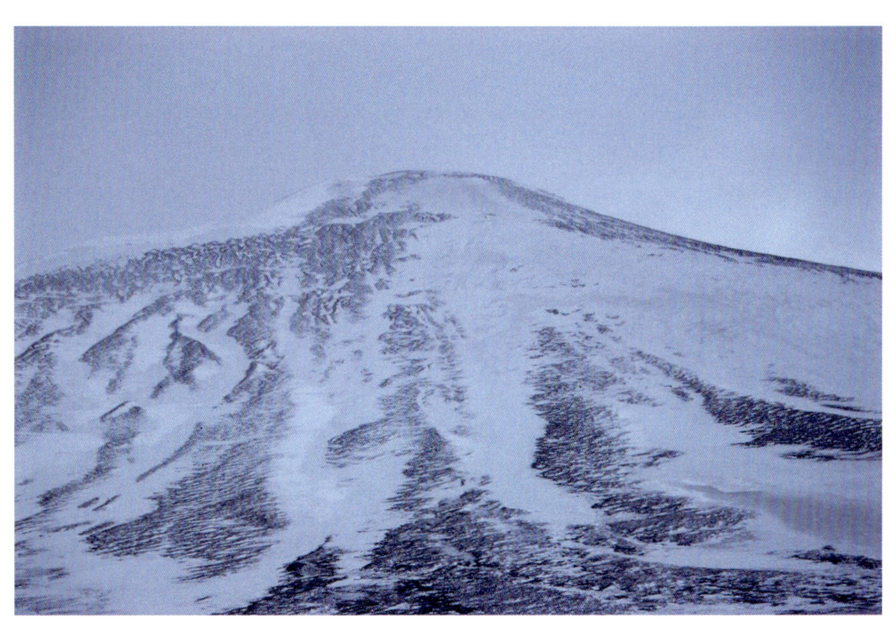

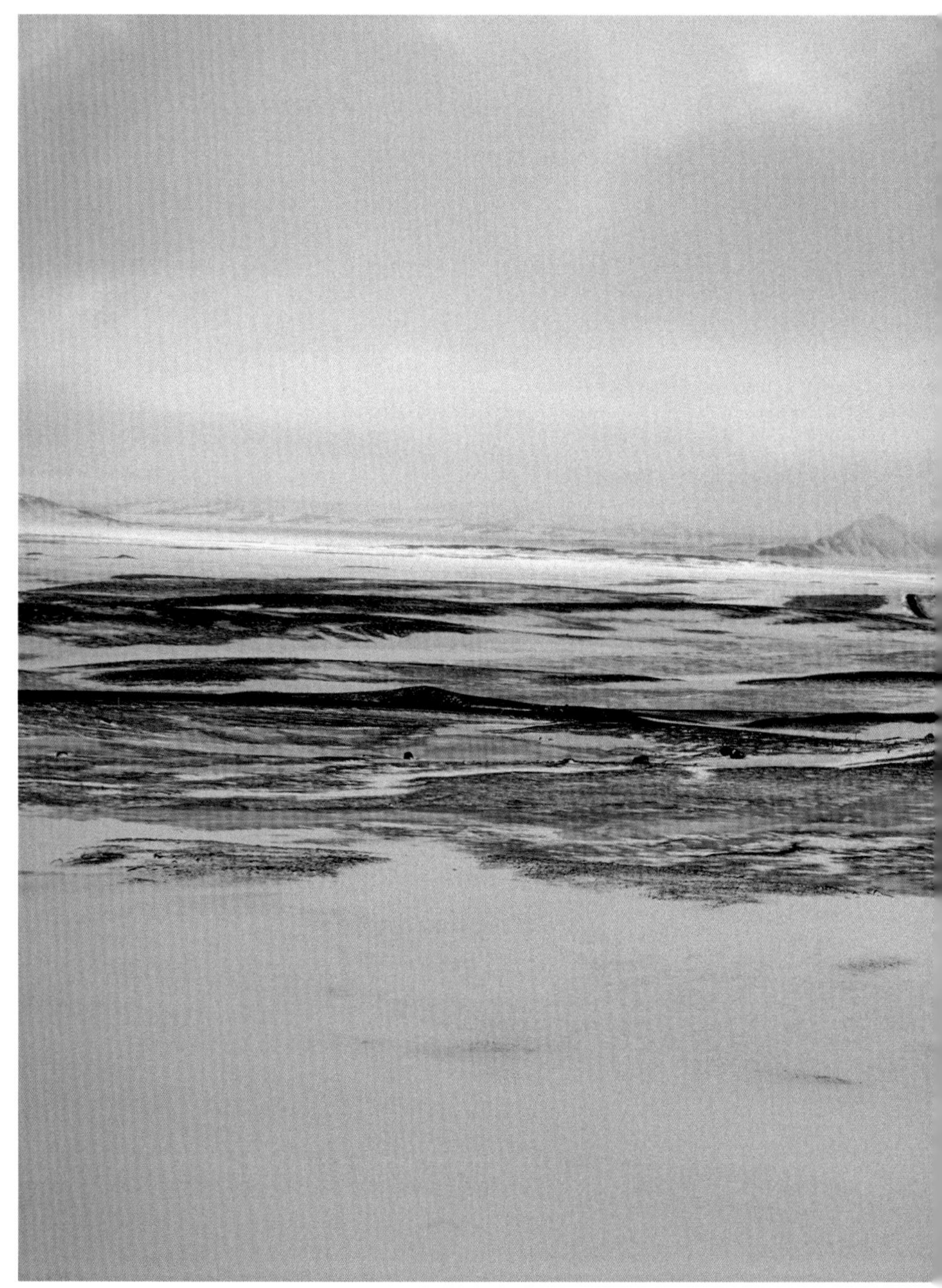

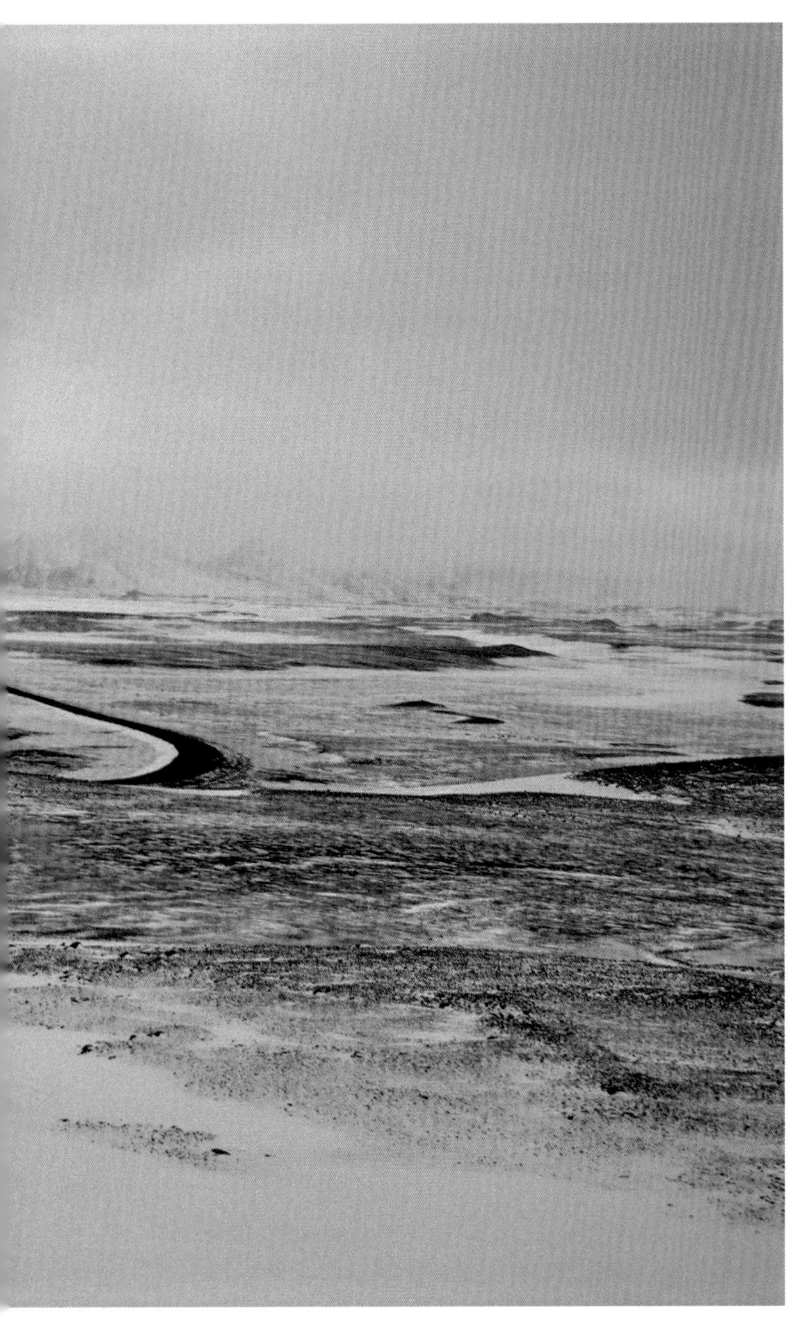

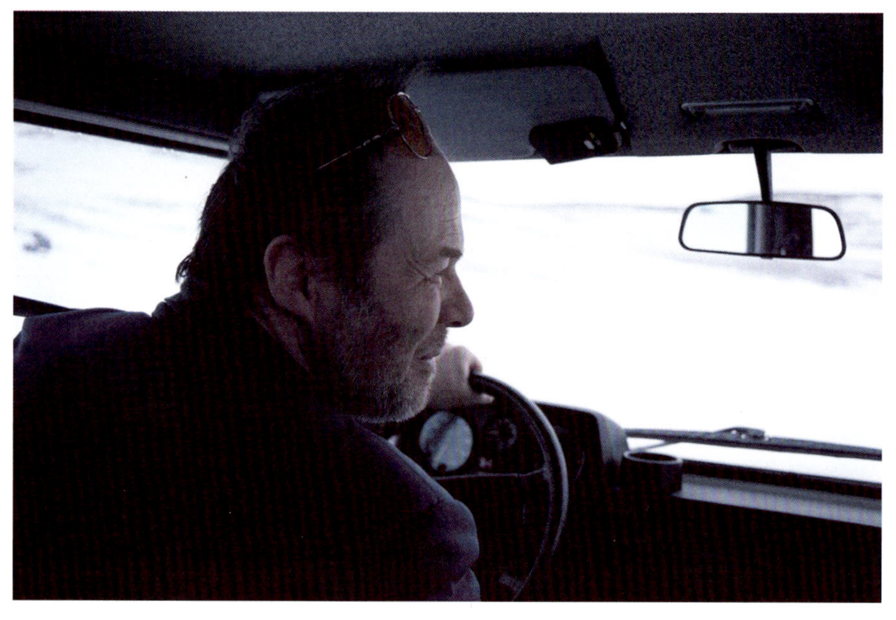

Jan Voss auf dem Weg nach Hjalteyri, 16. Februar 1997.
Jan Voss on the way to Hjalteyri, 16 February 1997.

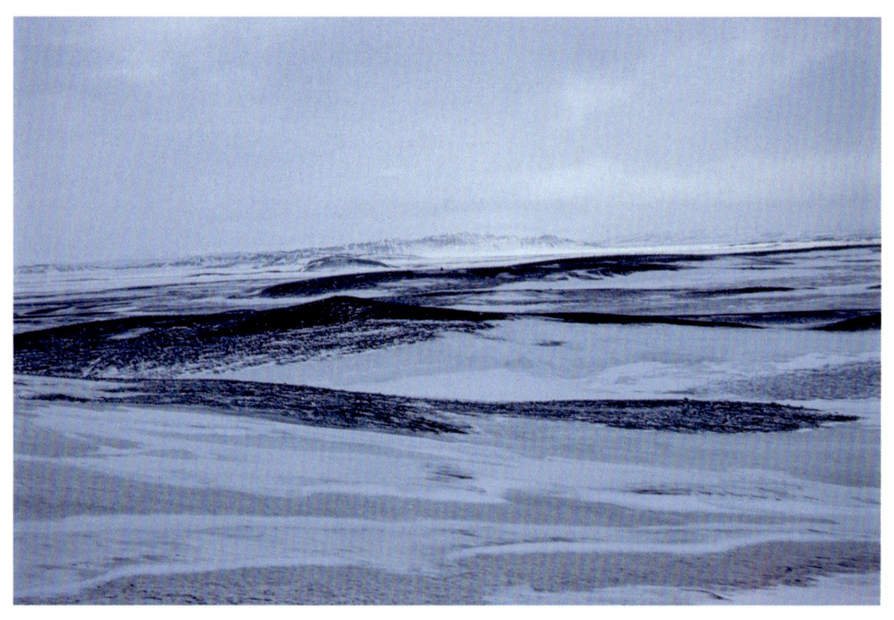

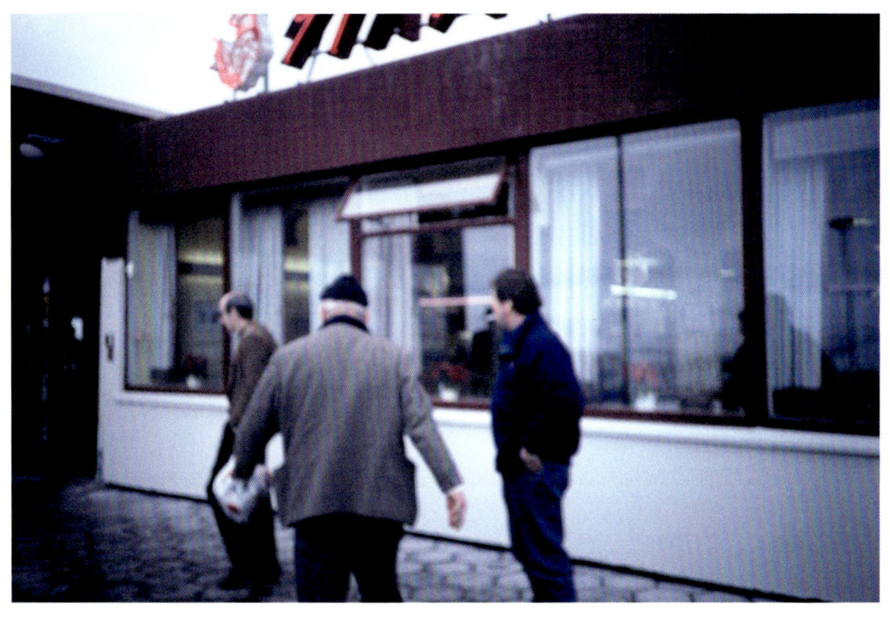

Beat Keusch, Dieter Roth und Gunnar Helgason in Akureyri, 17. Februar 1997.
Beat Keusch, Dieter Roth, and Gunnar Helgason in Akureyri, 17 February 1997.

Am 5. Juni 1998 erwartete ich Dieter Roth mit seiner Nichte
Yvonne Roth und Birgith Bühlmann, in deren Fotokopierladen er vom 13. März bis 30. Mai 1998 die Werkserie *Blumensträusse* gezeigt hatte, im Restaurant ‹Chez Donati› zum
Mittagessen. Als Dieter Roth zum Tisch kam, missfiel ihm die
Lithographie von Joan Miró, die direkt neben uns an der
Wand hing. Ich schlug vor, den Tisch zu wechseln. Darauf sagte
er: «Wir lassen uns von diesem Kerl nicht vertreiben» und
zeichnete eine Kopie des Bildes, mit der wir den Miró verdeckten. Marianne Huber vom ‹Chez Donati› bemerkte die Szene
und machte zwei Fotos, wahrscheinlich die letzten von
Dieter Roth, denn am Abend desselben Tages ist er in seinem
Atelier an der Hegenheimerstrasse 24 in Basel gestorben. Zwei
Tage später schrieb mir Marianne Huber, wie ich die Idee
fände, das Restaurant mit Werken von Dieter Roth voll zu hängen. Darauf installierten Björn Roth und ich eine Ausstellung.

At lunchtime on 5 June 1998, I sat waiting in the restaurant
Chez Donati for Dieter Roth, his niece Yvonne Roth, and
Birgith Bühlmann, whose photocopying shop had served as
a venue for the presentation of Dieter's work series *Flower
Bouquets* from 13 March to 30 May 1998. When Dieter stepped
up to the table, he exclaimed his dislike for the Joan Miró
lithograph on the wall next to our table. I suggested switching
tables, upon which he said, "no, we're not going to let this
guy drive us away." Instead, he sketched a copy of Miró's
picture and used it to cover the original work. Marianne Huber
of Chez Donati had noticed the scene and took two photographs, probably the last photographs of Dieter Roth, for
on that same evening Dieter Roth died in his studio at Hegenheimerstrasse 24 in Basel. Two days later, Marianne Huber
wrote to me and asked what I thought of the idea of hanging
the restaurant with works of Dieter Roth, upon which
Björn Roth and I mounted an exhibition at Chez Donati.

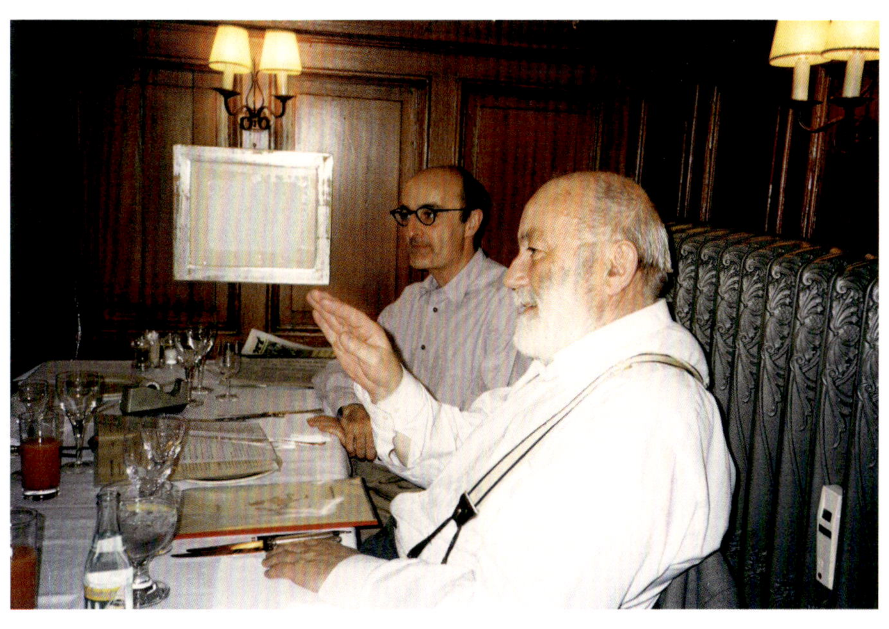

Restaurant ‹Chez Donati›, Basel, 5. Juni 1998.
    Restaurant Chez Donati, Basel, 5 June 1998.

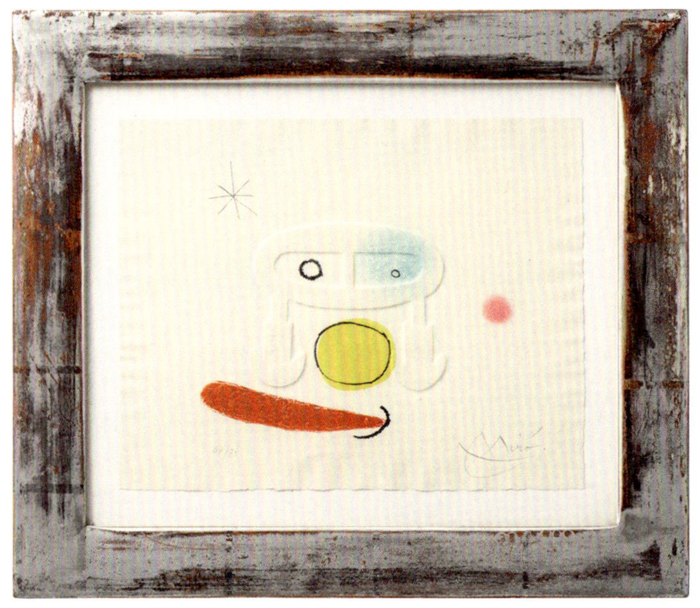

Joan Miró

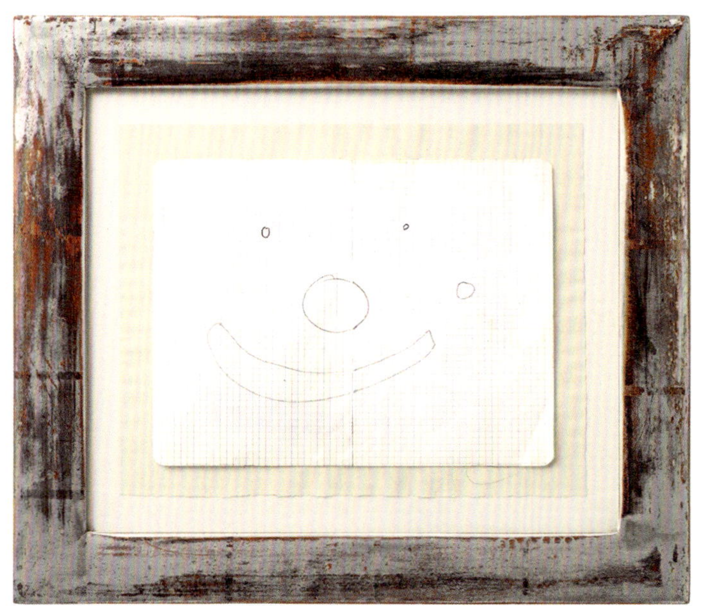

Dieter Roth

Dieter Roth-Ausstellung im Restaurant ‹Chez Donati›, 10. Juni bis 30. August 1998.
Dieter Roth exhibition at Restaurant Chez Donati, 10 June to 30 August 1998.

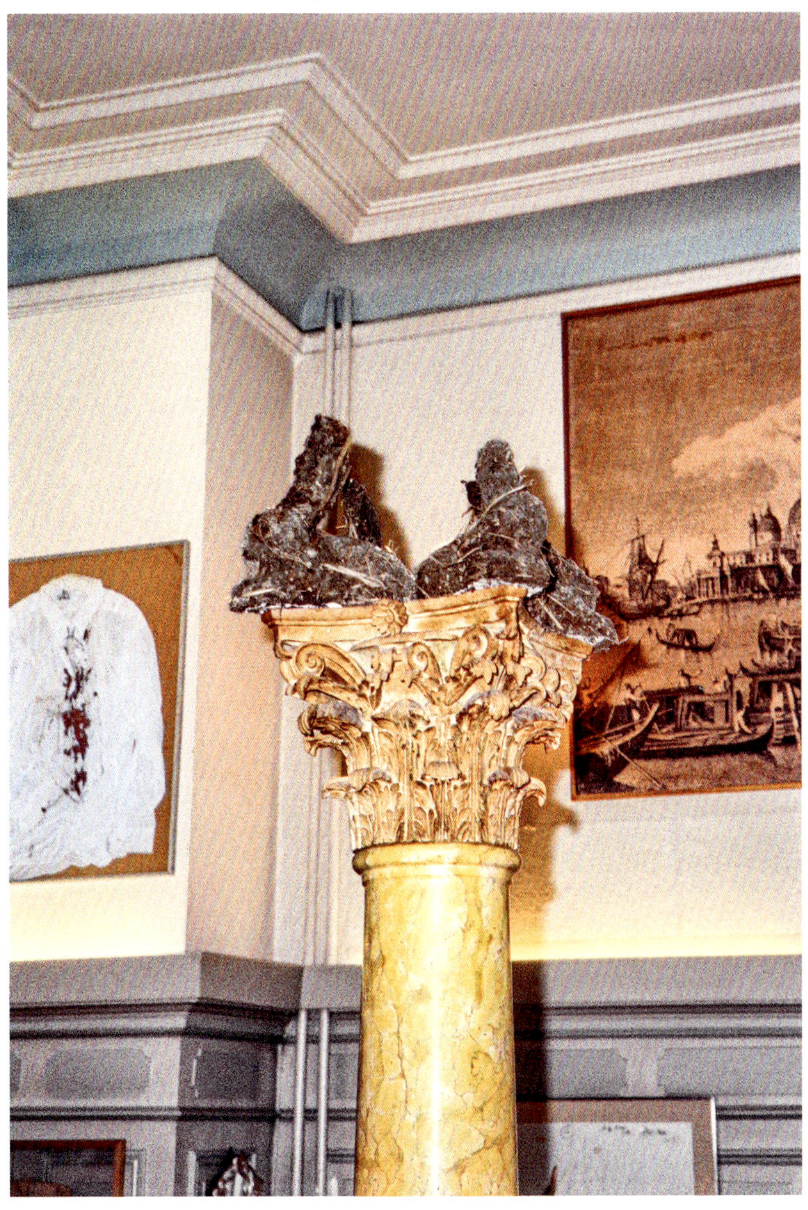

4 *Karnickelköttelkarnickel,* Kaninchenköttel, Stroh.
4 *RabbitPoopRabbits,* rabbit poops, straw.

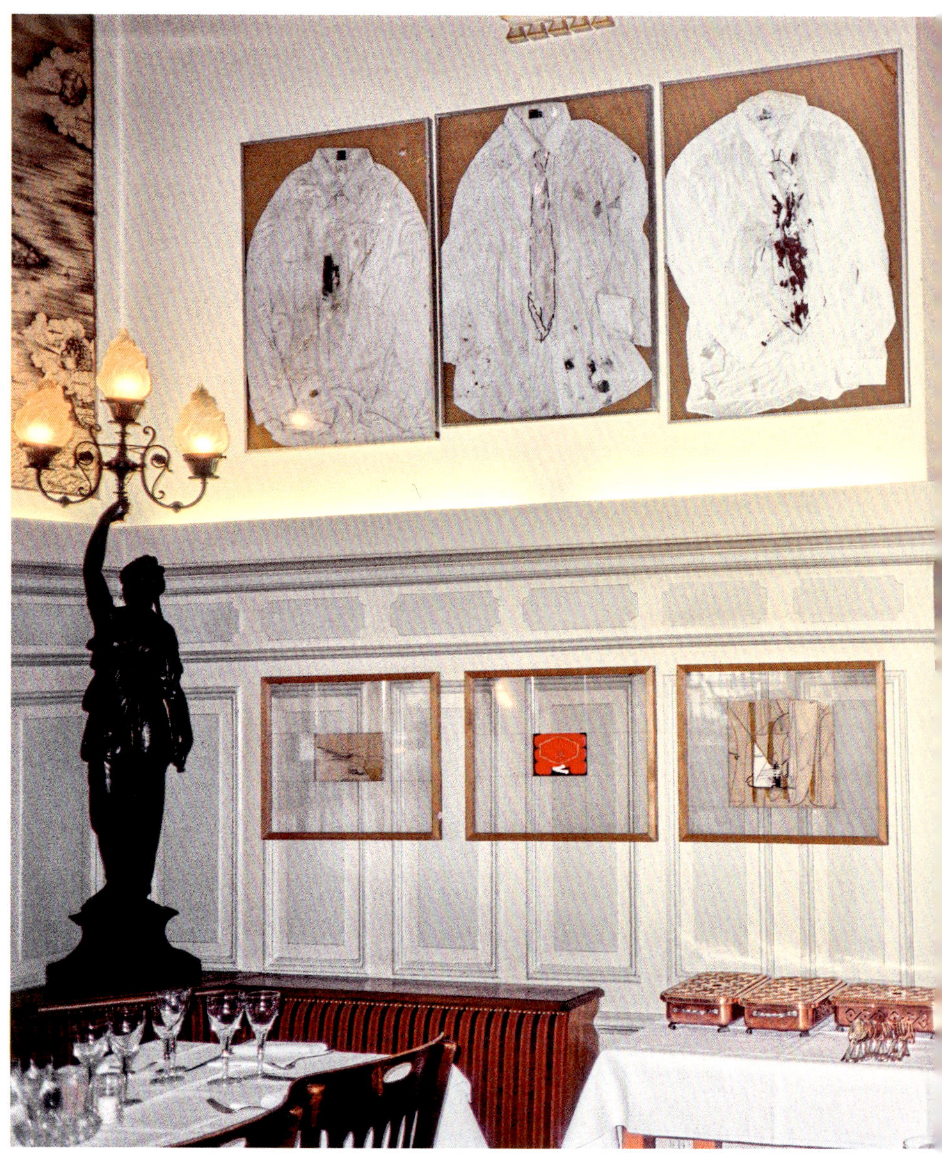

Oben: *Hemden,* 3 Materialbilder, Hemden, Acrylfarbe.
Unten: 3 Postkarten, Pappe, Acrylfarbe.
    Above: *Shirts,* 3 material pictures, shirts, acrylic paint.
    Below: 3 postcards, cardboard, acrylic paint.

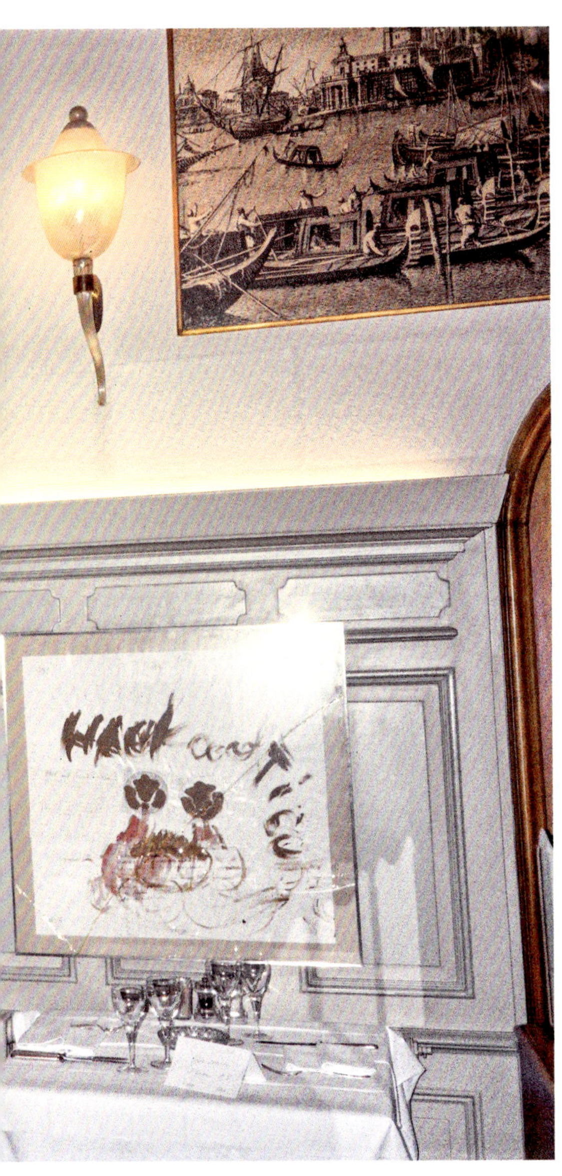

Stuttgarter Bilderbogen Nr. 12, Manuskript mit Collage,
Acrylfarbe, Filzstift, Bleistift.
Stuttgart Pictorial Broadsheet no 12, manuscript with collage,
acrylic paint, felt-tip pen, pencil.

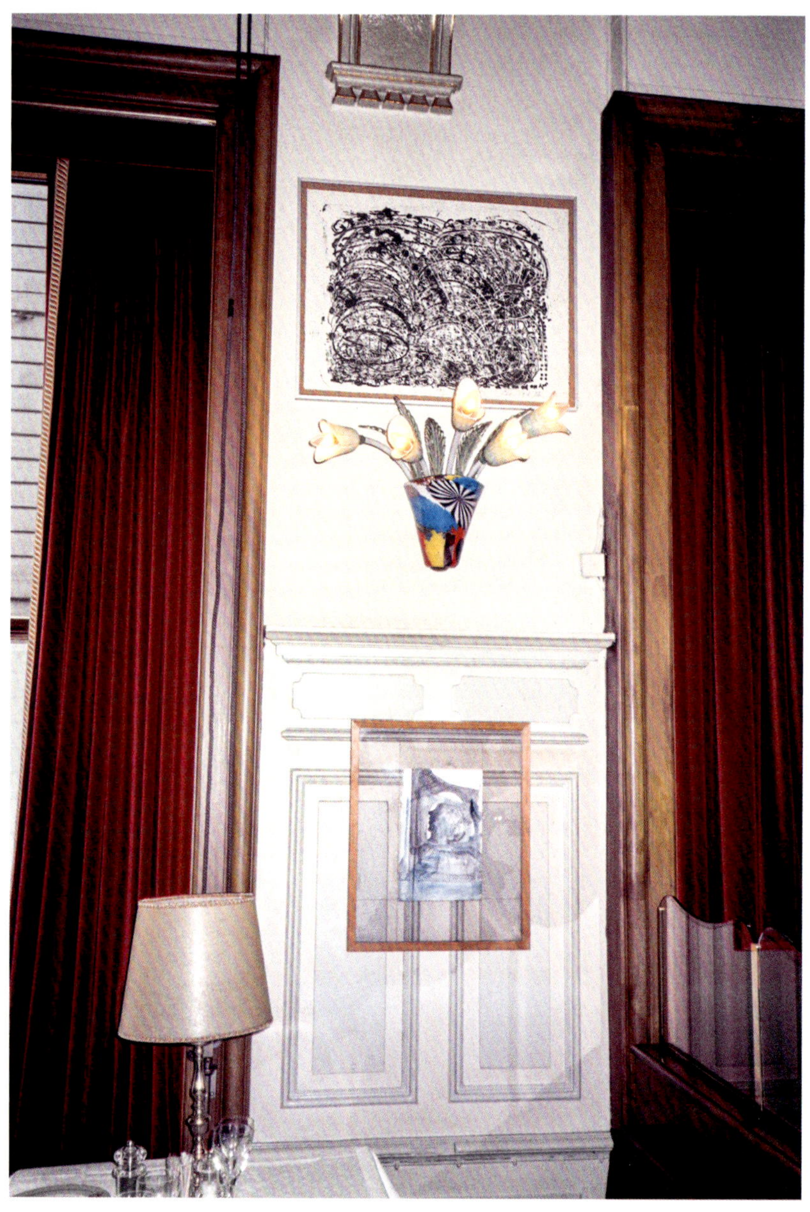

Oben: *Porzellanstein II,* Flachdruck (Stein). Unten: Postkarte, Pappe, Acrylfarbe.
Above: *Porcelain Stone II,* lithograph (stone). Below: postcard, cardboard, acrylic paint.

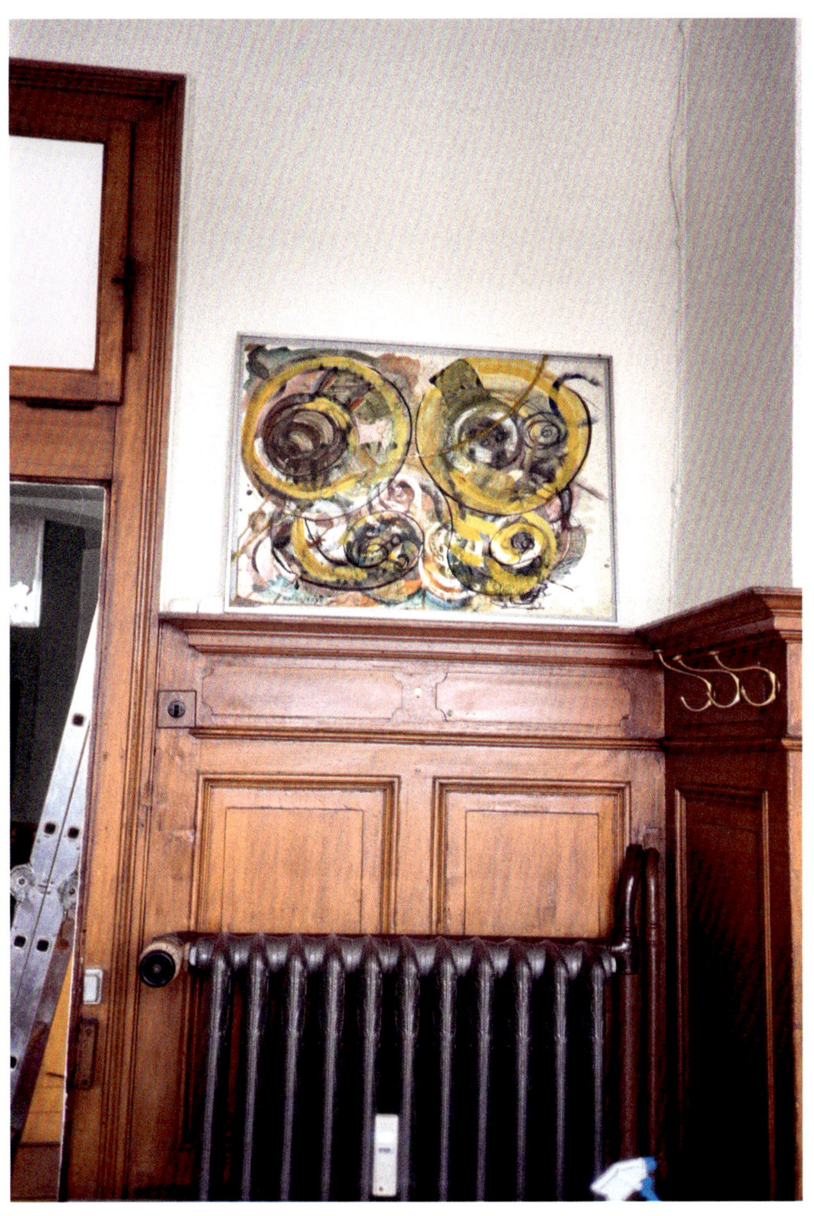

Waldhörner (mit Björn Roth), Acrylfarbe, Wasserfarbe, Farbkreide, Bleistift, Tusche.
Hunting Horns (with Björn Roth), acrylic paint, watercolour, crayon, pencil, Indian ink.

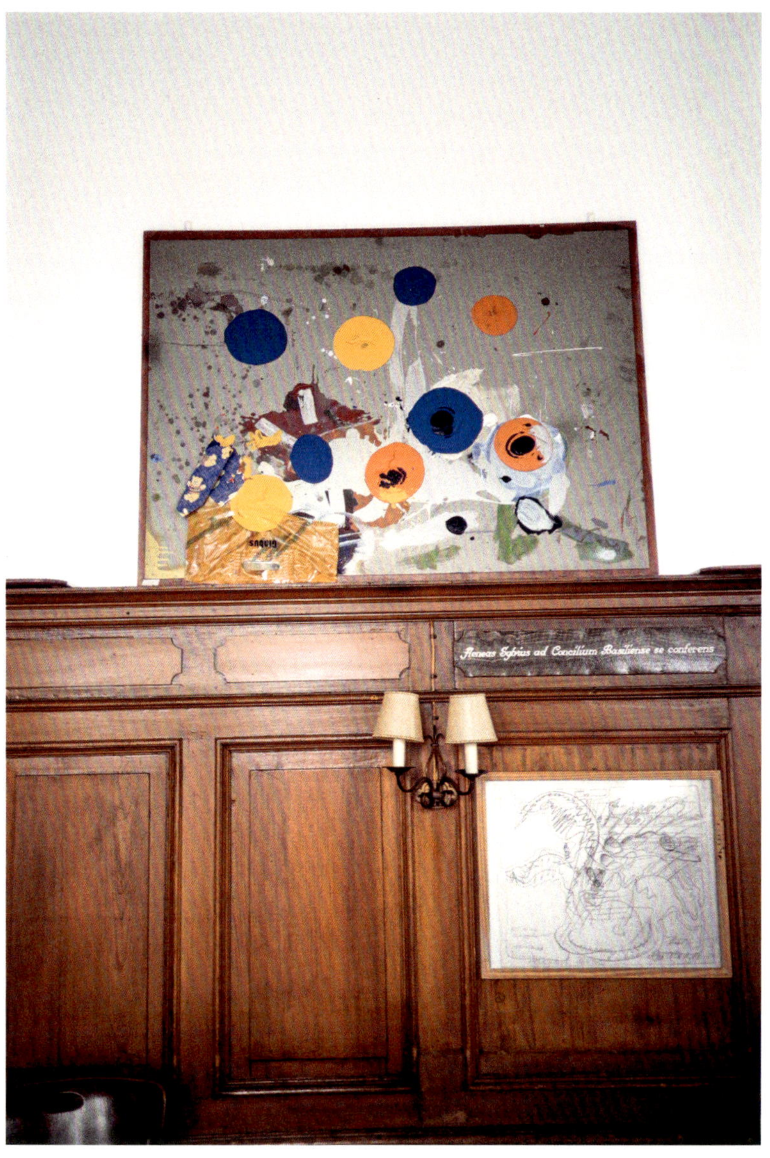

Oben: *Forcierte Matte: Abandonnements-Etüde,* Acrylfarbe, Tinte, Bleistift, Mattlack, Kleber, Collage. Unten: Bleistiftzeichnung.
    Above: *Laboured Desk Mat: Abandonment Study,* acrylic paint, ink, pencil, matt lacquer, glue, collage. Below: Pencil drawing.

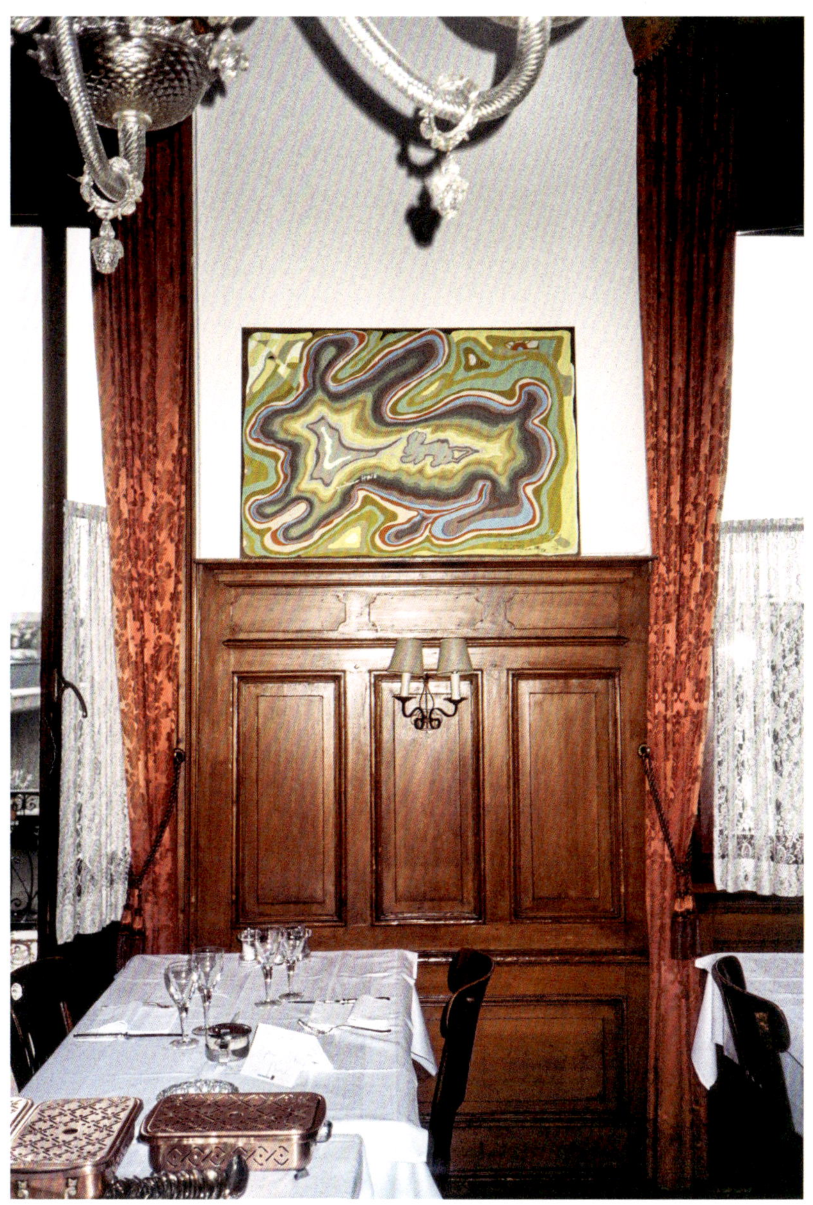

Ein gerissener Hase, Siebdruck in 28 Farben.
  A Cunning Rabbit, screen print in 28 colours.

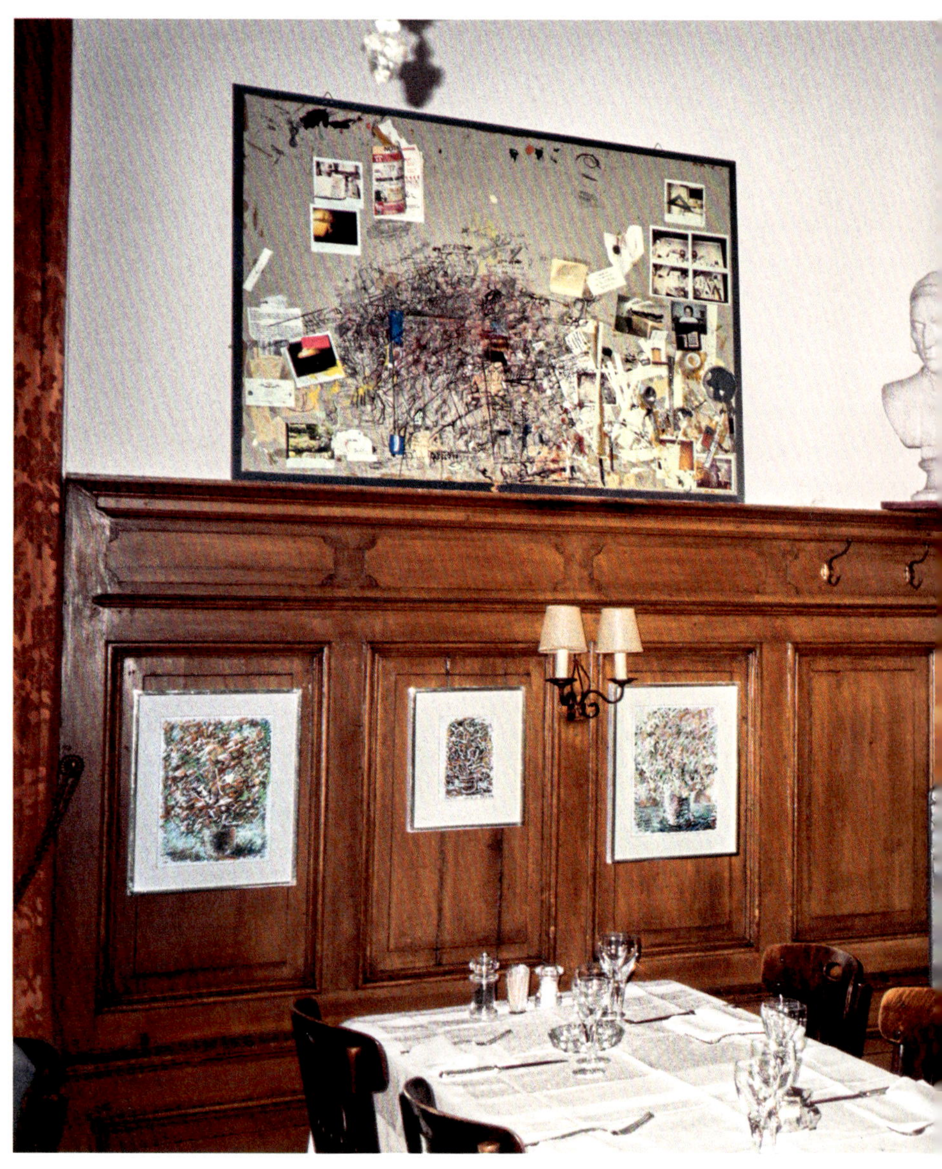

Oben: *Forcierte Matte* und *1. Forcierte Matte,* Acrylfarbe, Ölfarbe, Tinte, Fettkreide, Bleistift, Collage, Polaroids. Unten: *Blumensträusse,* 3 übermalte Farbkopien.
Above: *Laboured Desk Mat* and *1st Laboured Desk Mat,* acrylic paint, oil paint, ink, fatty chalk, pencil, collage, polaroid photos. Below: *Flower Bouquets,* 3 overpainted colour copies.

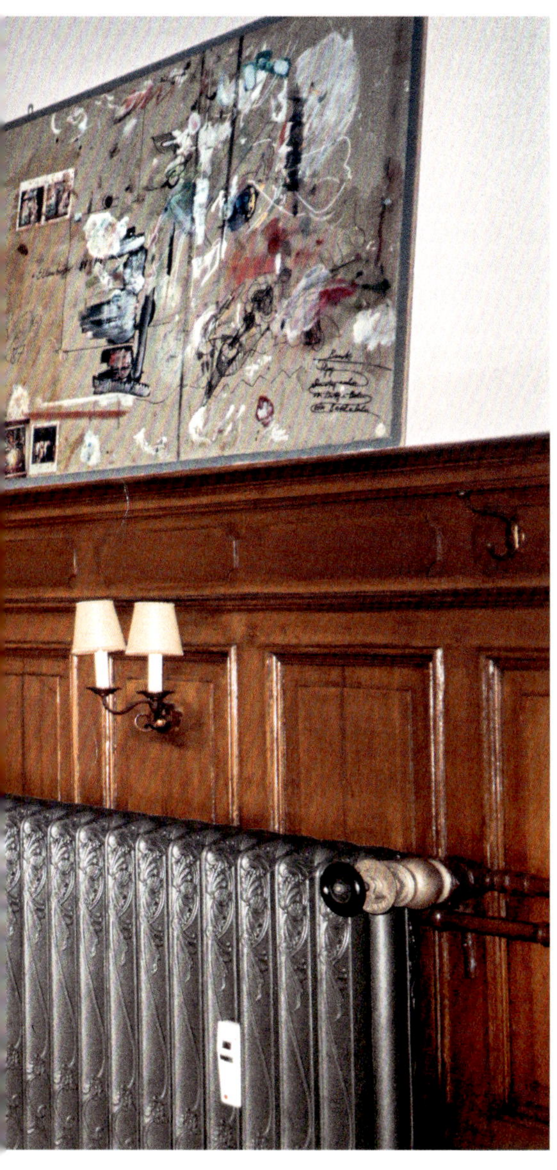

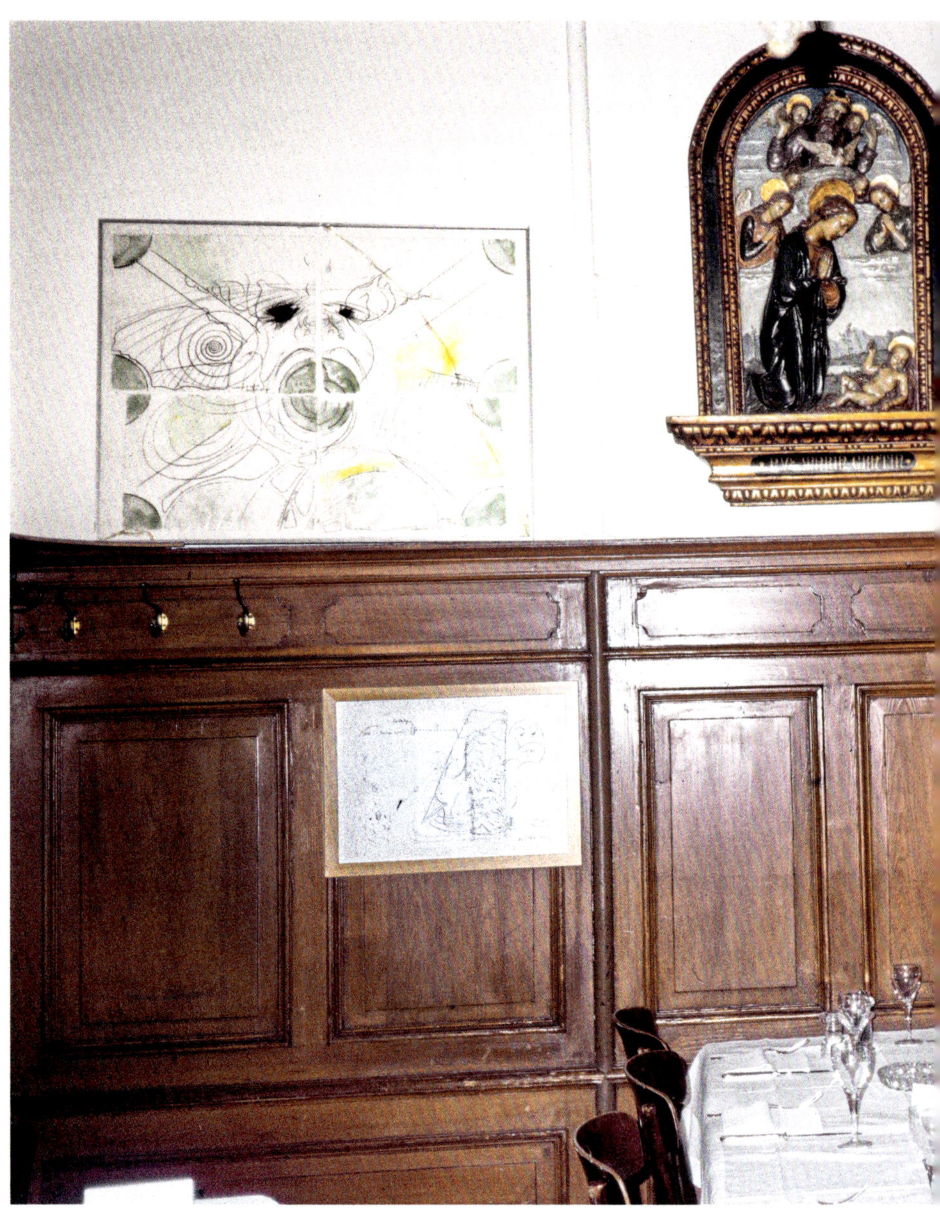

Oben: Bleistiftzeichnung, Acrylfarbe. Unten: Bleistiftzeichnungen.
Above: Pencil drawing, acrylic paint. Bellow: Pencil drawings.

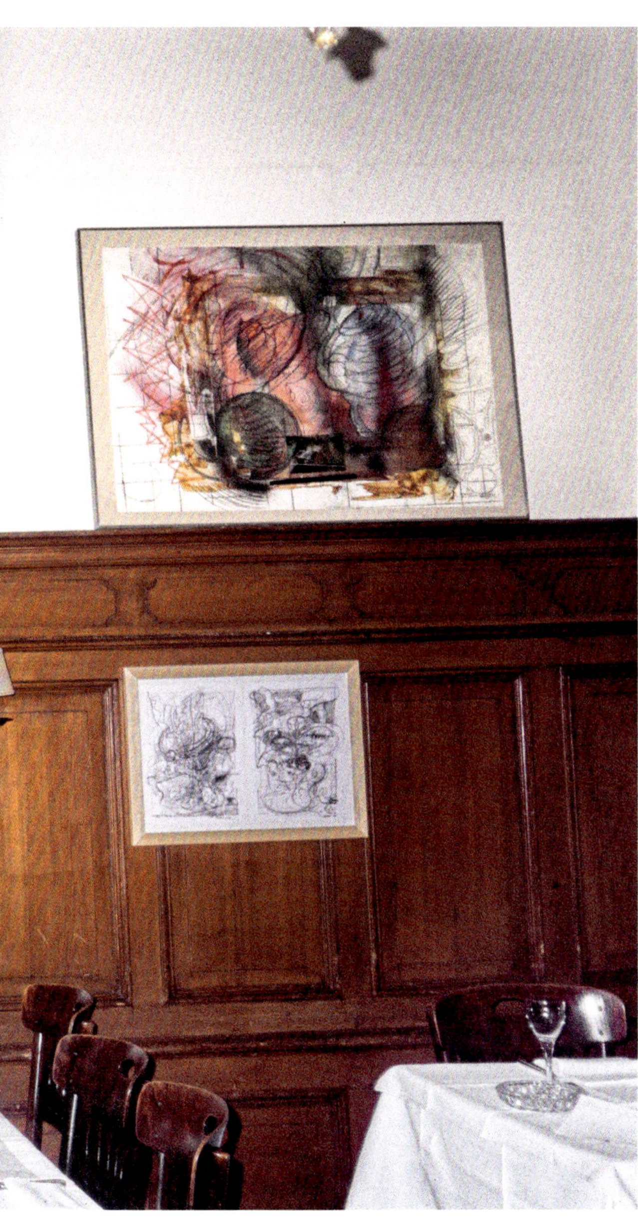

Oben: Bleistiftzeichnung übermalt (mit Björn Roth), Collage, Acrylfarbe, Tusche.
Above: Pencil drawing overpainted (with Björn Roth), collage, acrylic paint, Indian ink.

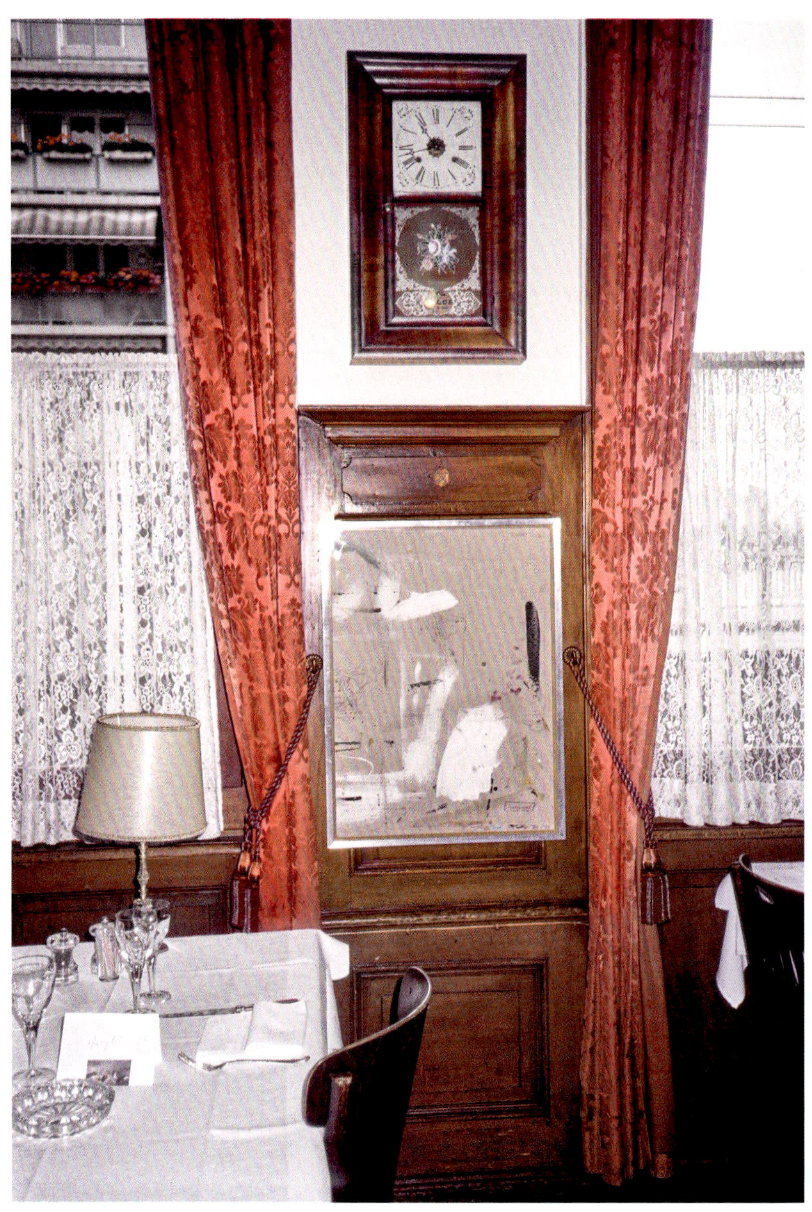

Matte, Bleistift, Tusche, Acrylfarbe.
　　Mat, pencil, Indian ink, acrylic paint.

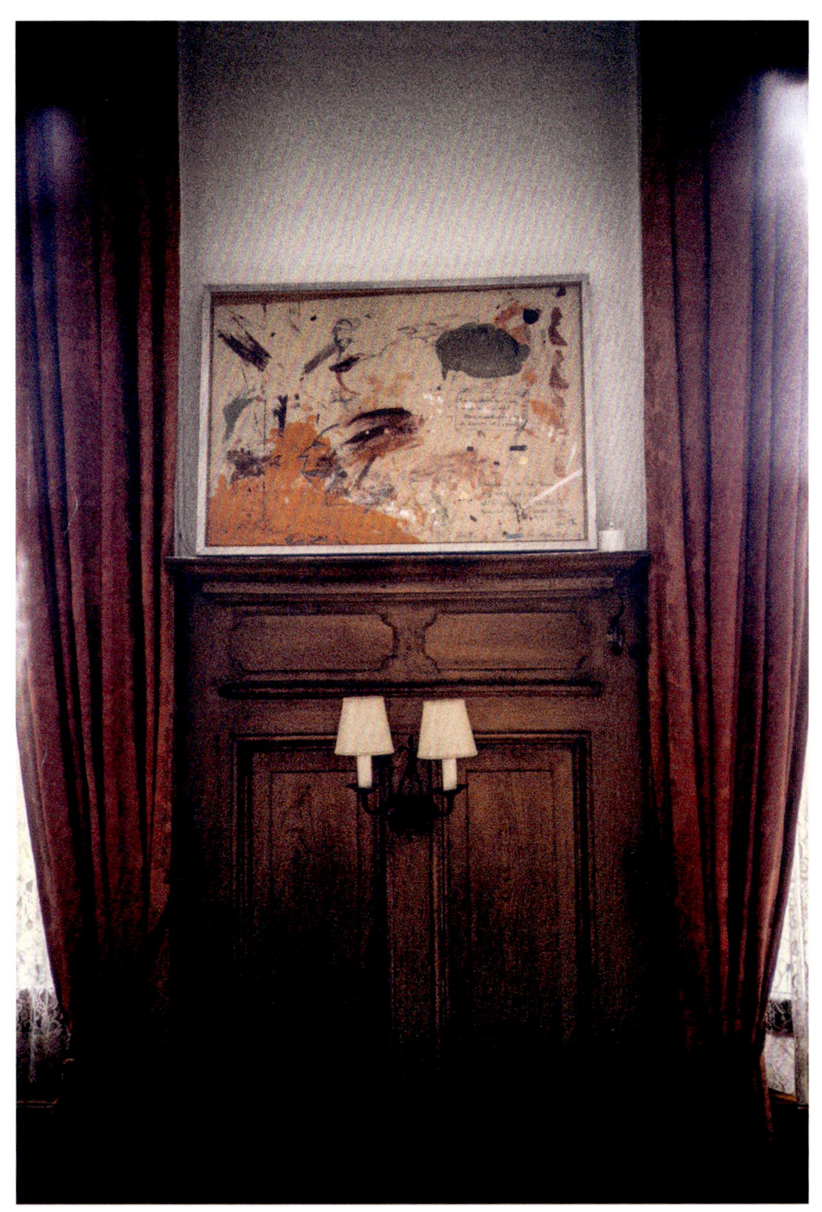

Bö-Matte (mit Björn Roth), Bleistift, Tusche, Acrylfarbe.
Bö Mat (with Björn Roth), pencil, Indian ink, acrylic paint.

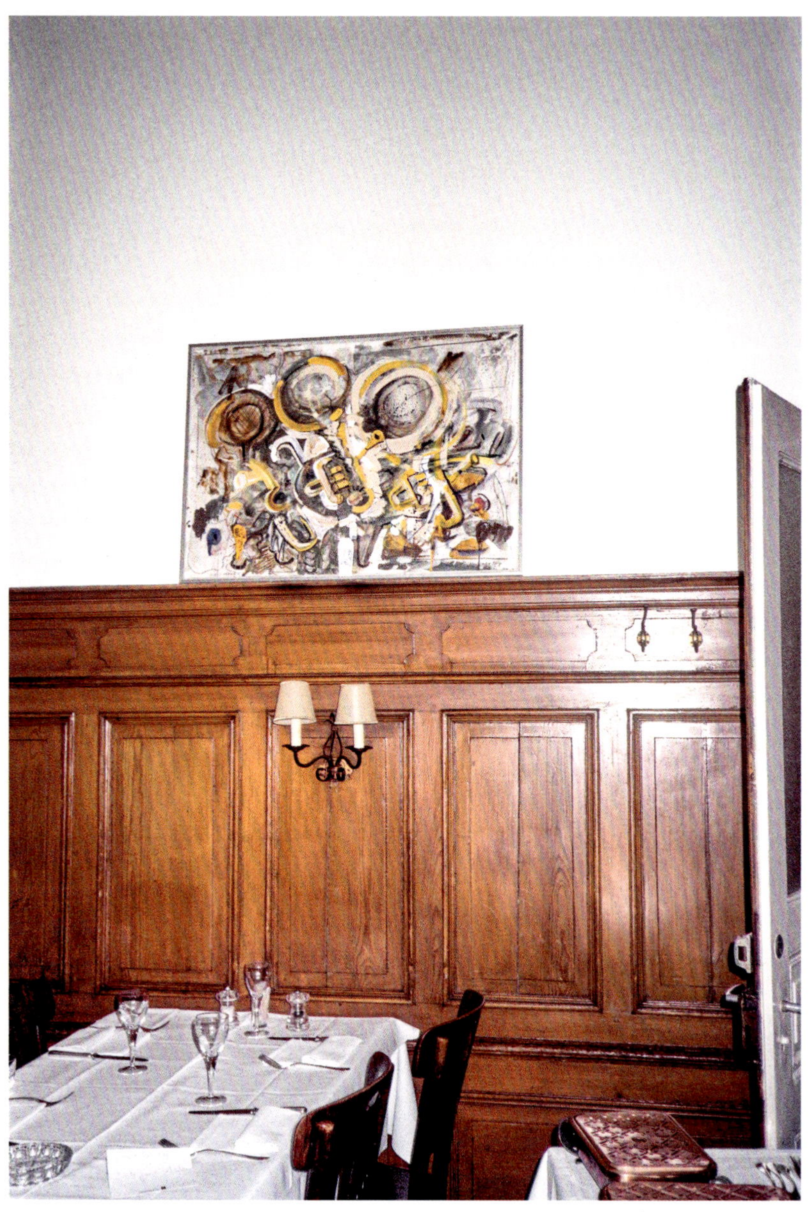

Waldhörner (mit Björn Roth), Acrylfarbe, Wasserfarbe, Farbkreide, Bleistift, Tusche.
Hunting Horns (with Björn Roth), acrylic paint, watercolour, crayon, pencil, Indian ink.

Neben Dieter Roths häufigen Kaffeebestellungen aus Island
stand manchmal auch ein Satz wie «Die Zeit vergeht, das
Leben scheints ebenso, o.k.?».

To his regular orders for coffee from Iceland, Dieter Roth
occasionally added short phrases, such as "Time passes, so
does life, it seems, okay?"

Dear Beat, Thanks!
(No trace of annoyance or disturbance)
Time passes, so does life, it seems, okay?
Dieterli
P.S. Coffee's arrived! Expect a faxilian call
for more soon – how about that?
Bali, 4 June 1996

Lieber Beat, Dankeschön!
(Nichts an Ärgernis noch Störnis)

Die Zeit vergeht, das Leben scheints
ebenso, o. K. ?

                              Dieterli

____

P.S: Kaffee hier !
Bald kommt der Ruf, der faxige, nach
mehr — wie wäre das ?

                    Bali,   4. Juni 1996

Dieter Roth, 1930 geboren in Hannover, 1998 gestorben in Basel, lebte in Deutschland, der Schweiz, in Island, Österreich und in den USA. Er schuf Gedichte, Prosatexte, Zeichnungen, Collagen, Materialbilder, Druckgraphiken, Künstlerbücher, Designobjekte, Skulpturen, Fotos, Filme, Musik. Und damit einen virtuosen Tatsachenbericht über unser Dasein.

Dieter Roth, born in Hanover in 1930, deceased in Basel in 1998, lived alternatively in Germany, Switzerland, Iceland, Austria, and the United States. He created poems and prose, drawings, collages, material pictures, prints, artist books, objects, sculptures, photographs, films, and music, thus offering a vivid account of our existence as human beings.

Wir danken Björn Roth und Jan Voss.
    We thank Björn Roth and Jan Voss.

Konzeption und Texte / Concept and texts: Beat Keusch
Lektorat und Korrektorat / Copyediting and proofreading: Doris Tranter
Übersetzung / Translation: Nigel Stephenson
Gestaltung / Graphic design: BKVK
Fotografien / Photographs: Beat Keusch, Erika Streit
Fotografie S. 101 / Photograph p. 101: Marianne Huber
Fotografien S. 102, 103 / Photographs p. 102, 103: Christoph Kern
Lithografie / Lithography: Georg Sidler
Papier / Paper: Gmund Colors Matt 34, 135 g/m² Magno Volume 1.05
Schrift / Typeface: SangBleu Republic
Druck / Printing: Offsetdruckerei Grammlich, Graffiti Siebdruck
Bindung / Binding: Idupa Schübelin

Zitat S. 11 / Quotation p. 11: Aus dem Nachwort von /
from the afterword by Jan Voss in «Dieter Roth, Da drinnen vor dem Auge»,
S. 299 / p. 299. © Suhrkamp Verlag
Zeichnung S. 71 / Drawing p. 71: Im Besitz von / in the possession of
Beat Keusch, Erika Streit

Distribution worldwide by
Hatje Cantz Verlag GmbH
Mommsenstraße 27
10629 Berlin
Germany
www.hatjecantz.com
A Ganske Publishing Group Company

ISBN 978-3-7757-5116-2

Printed in Germany

Weiterführend:

– *Wahn. Sinn. Kunst. Müll. Dieter Roth in der Fabrik.* Du, Heft Nr. 6, Juni 1993
– *Dieter Roth. Melancholischer Nippes / Frühe Objekte und Materialbilder
  1960–1975*, ergänzt und kommentiert von Dieter Roth. Dirk Dobke (Hg.),
  2 Bände, Verlag der Buchhandlung Walther König, 2002
– *Dieter Roth. Gesammelte Interviews.* Barbara Wien (Hg.),
  Edition Hansjörg Mayer, 2002
– *Dieter Roth. Originale.* Dieter Roth Foundation / Dirk Dobke (Hg.),
  Edition Hansjörg Mayer, 2002
– *Roth-Zeit. Eine Dieter Roth Retrospektive.* Theodora Vischer,
  Bernadette Walter (Hg.), Lars Müller Publishers, 2003
– *Dieter Roth. Da drinnen vor dem Auge. Lyrik und Prosa.*
  Jan Voss, Beat Keusch, Johannes Ullmaier, Björn Roth (Hg.), edition suhrkamp, 2005
– *Dieter Roth Puzzle.* Film von Hilmar Oddsson, 2008
– *Dieter Roth Souvenirs.* Beat Keusch, Dieter Roth Akademie (Hg.),
  Hatje Cantz, 2011
– Schimmelmuseum: www.dieterrothmuseum.org/schimmelmuseum
– Roth-Raum: www.schaulager.org/de/fuehrung-roth
– Mehr Bücher: www.boekiewoekie.com

Further reading:

– *Dieter Roth Academy. Til Dæmis And Whatsoe'er.* Compiled by Björn Roth and Jan Voss,
  Dieter Roth Academy, Roth's Verlag – Boekie Woekie, books by artists, 2001
– *Dieter and Dorothy.* Dorothy Iannone (ed.), bilgerverlag, 2001
– *Dieter Roth. Unique Pieces.* Dieter Roth Foundation / Dirk Dobke (eds.),
  Edition Hansjörg Mayer, 2002
– *Dieter Roth Academy. Conference in Seyðisfjörður, May 2002.* Dieter Roth Academy (ed.),
  Roth's Verlag – Boekie Woekie, books by artists, 2003
– *Roth Time. A Dieter Roth Retrospective.* Theodora Vischer,
  Bernadette Walter (eds.), Lars Müller Publishers, 2004
– *Dieter Roth Puzzle.* Film by Hilmar Oddsson, 2008
– *Dieter Roth Souvenirs.* Beat Keusch, Dieter Roth Academy (eds.),
  Hatje Cantz, 2011
– *Dieter Roth. Collected Interviews.* Barbara Wien (ed.),
  Edition Hansjörg Mayer, 2019
– Schimmelmuseum: www.dieterrothmuseum.org/en/moldmuseum
– Roth Room: www.schaulager.org/en/dieter-roth-guided-tours
– More Books: www.boekiewoekie.com

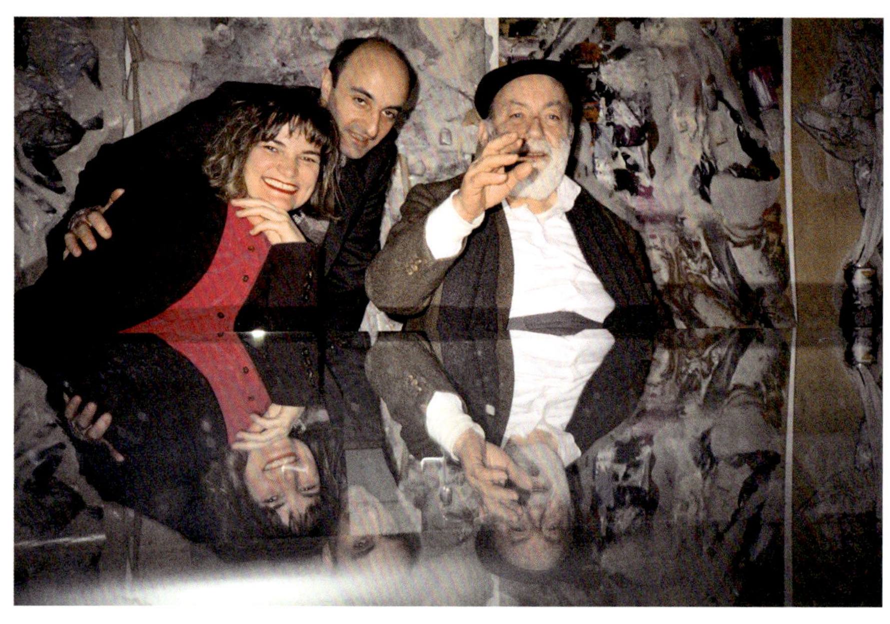

Erika Streit, Beat Keusch und Dieter Roth im ‹Dieter Roth Museum›,
Hamburg, 23. April 1994.
    Erika Streit, Beat Keusch, and Dieter Roth in the Dieter Roth Museum,
    Hamburg, 23 April 1994.